CBT and DBT Skills Mastery

Combat Overthinking, Anxiety and Stress with Effective CBT and DBT Tools. Overcome Negative Spirals and Stay Present

Linda Hill

© **Copyright 2023 - All rights reserved.**

The content contained within this book may not be reproduced, duplicated or transmitted without direct written permission from the author or the publisher.

Under no circumstances will any blame or legal responsibility be held against the publisher, or author, for any damages, reparation, or monetary loss due to the information contained within this book, either directly or indirectly.

Legal Notice:

This book is copyright protected. It is only for personal use. You cannot amend, distribute, sell, use, quote or paraphrase any part, or the content within this book, without the consent of the author or publisher.

Disclaimer Notice:

Please note the information contained within this document is for educational and entertainment purposes only. All effort has been executed to present accurate, up to date, reliable, complete information. No warranties of any kind are declared or implied. Readers acknowledge that the author is not engaged in the rendering of legal, financial, medical or professional advice. The content within this book has been derived from various sources. Please consult a licensed professional before attempting any techniques outlined in this book.

By reading this document, the reader agrees that under no circumstances is the author responsible for any losses, direct or indirect, that are incurred as a result of the use of the information contained within this document, including, but not limited to, errors, omissions, or inaccuracies.

Table of Contents

Introduction 1

Chapter 1: The Cognitive-Behavioral Toolkit 8
    CBT Basics 9
    How CBT Works 11
    CBT for Anxiety and Panic 12
    What Techniques Are Used in CBT? 12
    How Is CBT Different From Other Therapies? 17
    CBT and Individual Therapy 18
    CBT and Group Therapy 19
    CBT and Family Therapy 19
    How Long Does CBT Take? 19
    What Happens After CBT? 20
    Key Takeaways 20

Chapter 2: The Dialectical-Behavior Therapy Toolkit ... 21
    Basics of DBT 22

What Is DBT Used For? 24

How Is DBT Different From Other Therapies? 30

What Are the Benefits of DBT? 30

What Are the Risks of DBT? 30

DBT and Individual Therapy 31

DBT and Group Therapy 31

DBT and Family Therapy 31

Key Takeaways 32

Chapter 3: The Dual Power of CBT and DBT 33

Four Differences Between CBT and DBT 34

CBT Versus DBT Philosophies 34

DBT in Action: Dealing With Difficult Emotions 36

CBT in Action: Challenging Negative Thoughts 36

How Do I Know if CBT or DBT Is Better for Me? 37

DBT Modules Versus CBT Modules 38

How to Combine CBT and DBT 40

Pros and Cons of Combining CBT and DBT 43

CBT and DBT for Emotional Sensitivity 44

CBT and DBT for Emotional Distress 45

Key Takeaways 46

Chapter 4: Why Is Your Brain Against You? 48

Survival Triumphs Happiness 49

Brains Sabotage the Present Moment 52

How To Rewire Your Brain 56

Table of Contents

Neuroplasticity 57

Chapter 5: The Root of Anxiety, Worry, and Panic 59

What Is Anxiety? 60

What Is the Difference Between Anxiety and Worry? 60

What Is the Difference Between Anxiety and Panic? 61

What Are the Different Anxiety Disorders? 61

What Are the Symptoms of Anxiety? 62

How Is Anxiety Treated? 63

What Causes Anxiety? 63

What Are Some Tips for Managing Anxiety? 67

Identifying the Root of Your Anxiety 68

Keep a Kind and Open-Minded Mindset 73

Befriend Your Anxiety 79

Key Takeaways 83

Chapter 6: Emotional Numbness 85

What Is Emotional Numbness? 86

Symptoms of Emotional Numbness 86

Causes of Emotional Numbness 87

How to Cope With Emotional Numbness 89

Treating Emotional Numbness 94

Additional Coping Tips 94

DBT and CBT Techniques That Can Help 97

Key Takeaways 98

Chapter 7: Rogue Emotions 100

What Are Rogue Emotions?.. 101

What Are the Symptoms of Rogue Emotions?............................. 102

What Are the Causes of Rogue Emotions? 103

What Are the Treatments for Rogue Emotions?.......................... 103

What Is Emotional Sensitivity?.. 113

What Are the Symptoms of Emotional Sensitivity?..................... 114

What Are the Treatments for Emotional Sensitivity?................... 114

Being Sensitive to Emotional Stimuli 115

Adapting to Emotional Stimuli 116

What Is Emotional Distress?... 117

Warning and Risk Factors of Emotional Distress 118

Can You Experience Both Rogue Emotions and Emotional Numbness?... 123

Key Takeaways 124

Chapter 8: The Danger Zone 126

What Is the Danger Zone? 127

How Do You Get Into the Danger Zone?.................................... 127

Why Does the Danger Zone Exist?.. 128

What Are the Symptoms of the Danger Zone? 130

What Are the Consequences of the Danger Zone?...................... 132

What Can You Do if You Are in the Danger Zone? 134

How Can You Prevent the Danger Zone? 138

Why Is Prevention Important? 138

How Can DBT and CBT Skills Help Me With the Danger Zone?...... 140

Table of Contents

What Do I Need to Do to Get Out of or Prevent Entering the
Danger Zone? 140

Key Takeaways 142

Chapter 9: There's Nothing to Worry About 144

Thought Distortions 149

Overcoming Thought Distortions 153

Key Takeaways 156

Chapter 10: Experience Is Your Guru 158

Experience by Doing 159

Experience By Reflecting 161

Making It a Habit 162

Why Is Experience Important? 163

Making the Most of Experience 164

Measuring Your Success 165

Tips for Success 166

Key Takeaways 167

Chapter 11: You Are Not Alone 168

The Importance of Socializing 169

CBT and Socializing 170

DBT and Socializing 171

Key Takeaways 175

Chapter 12: Breath in Peace, Exhale and Let Go 176

What Is Mindfulness? 177

How to Practice Mindfulness 179

Mindfulness-Based Techniques for Managing Emotions 182

CBT and Mindfulness 184

Key Takeaways 185

Conclusion 187

Thank You 192

The Ultimate Guide to Cognitive Behavioral Therapy 193

References 194

Introduction

Nothing diminishes anxiety faster than action.
—Walter Anderson

Do you feel caught up in the emotional whirlwind of your thoughts and feelings? Do you feel like your emotions are controlling you and you can't control them? Is your mental health affecting your day-to-day life? If you answered yes to any of these questions, you may benefit from learning how to control and better manage your emotions.

Many people struggle to keep their emotions in check. But there is hope! Cognitive-behavioral therapy (CBT) is a type of therapy that can help you understand and manage your emotions by understanding your thoughts. Dialectical behavior therapy (DBT) was derived from CBT and specifically focuses on helping you regulate your emotions. In this workbook, you will learn the basic principles of each therapy technique and how to apply them in your everyday life.

In my childhood, I was a fairly cheerful kid. I had friends, did well in school, and was involved in extracurricular activities. However, when I entered my teenage years, things changed. I became withdrawn and depressed. I didn't want to see my friends or do anything that I used to enjoy. My grades slipped, and I stopped going to school. It felt like the light had gone out of my life. At first, my parents chalked it up to normal teenage angst and a phase I would "grow out of."

However, my behavior only got worse. I hated disappointing my parents, but I also lacked the ambition to break the cycle. So, my parents took me to see a therapist, who, instead of teaching me coping techniques, put me on medication. The medication didn't fix the root of the problem. In fact, I often felt worse within hours of swallowing those big pills.

I noticed I started suffering from other problems, such as emotional numbness. For my sixteenth birthday, my family planned a surprise party for me. They were proud of the steps I was taking to improve myself, but I wasn't as impressed. Instead of feeling thrilled and excited like they had hoped, I felt nothing. I felt like I was trapped in my body and was emotionless. My face almost always had a blank expression. A smile or a laugh looked and sounded fake. I couldn't even fool myself. My essence was trapped within myself, and I couldn't let it out.

However, if I forgot my medication, even for one day, I experienced the extreme opposite. I would become easily agitated, my heart would race, and I would get angry over the smallest things. One time, I even got into a fistfight with one of my friends. I felt like I was walking on eggshells, never knowing when I would explode or be apathetic and I knew my friends and family felt similarly.

When my grandmother, my best friend who always pushed me to be my best, died, I felt nothing, not even shedding a tear. On the other hand, one morning I forgot my medication, and I received a failing grade on an essay I worked hard on. For this, I cried for hours, feeling all the pain and hurt I had been numbing for months. It was then that I realized I needed help, that I couldn't keep living like this. The medication was only making the situation worse. If I wanted to progress, I needed a major change.

Internally, I questioned the therapist and her techniques. According to her, I was a "normal teenager" adjusting to "normal life" and just needed a little more "support along the way." However, the constant change from experiencing all the emotions at once to no emotions at all was taking a toll. Feeling like a zombie who was just navigating through life was more detrimental than experiencing the pains and failures of life. I was beginning to think something was really wrong with me.

Was I bipolar? Is that why I was experiencing dramatic extremes? Did I suffer from borderline personality disorder? Why were all the other people in my life so thrilled with their experiences while I was left unfulfilled? The therapist was unconvinced, but I still felt lost. I wanted to smile like everyone else, but instead, that's when I entered the "danger zone."

By the time I was seventeen, my anxiety was out of control. I couldn't bear to go to school for fear of interacting with others or having a teacher shine the spotlight on me. Going to the movies with friends was no longer an option because not only did I not have friends anymore, but going to the movies meant I would have to sit in a chair for two hours without moving, surrounded by strangers—something that was nearly impossible for me. I would often have full-blown anxiety attacks where my heart would race, I would sweat, and I couldn't breathe. It felt like the walls were tightening around me and I was about to die.

I was losing hope. The therapist kept telling my family and me that we needed to "give it time." Meanwhile, time seemed to be running out. With each day, it felt like I was slipping further and further away from the person I used to be. I no longer recognized myself. I was a shell of my former self—a ghost walking through life, barely living and barely hanging on.

That's when I took matters into my own hands. I started doing research on mental health and disorders. I read articles, books, and listened to popular therapists who shared different techniques for the challenges I was experiencing. I learned about different treatments and what worked for other people. The therapist I had wasn't helping me, so I stopped going to see her. I convinced my parents to pick a new therapist.

Within the first session, I noticed a vast difference. This therapist listened to me and didn't brush off my feelings. She encouraged me to talk about my experiences and asked questions about how I was feeling. Instead of throwing around "theories" or making assumptions, she let me lead the conversation. For the first time in a long time, I felt heard, like my feelings and experiences mattered. Eventually, I could open up about the things that were really bothering me.

I talked about my anxiety, my sadness, and the numbness I felt. What was different was that she provided me with hands-on experience to work on my emotions and behaviors. She also introduced me to a book called *The Dialectical Behavior Therapy Skills Workbook* by Matthew McKay, Jeffrey C. Wood, and Jeffrey Brantley. This book saved my life.

It introduced me to the concept of mindfulness and taught me how to be present in the moment. It also taught me how to cope with my emotions healthily. Instead of just listening to my therapist and doing what she said, she let me practice the skills I was learning in our sessions. The book has helped me immensely. Since reading this book and implementing the skills I learned, I could regulate my emotions and live a "normal" life.

In my senior year, my parents, teachers, and therapist all noticed a change in me. I was more engaged in school, participated regularly in class, and made friends again. I even got a part-time job. I could do these things because I had learned how to cope with my anxiety and emotions. When I got to college, I had this incessant need to learn more about myself and others who have suffered like me. I started reading psychology books and taking classes. It was then that I realized I wanted to pursue a career in mental health so that I could help others who were going through what I went through.

In today's society, people are a little more open and understanding about mental health. However, there's still a negative stigma that can surround mental illnesses and our emotions. I think it's important to talk about mental health to break the stigma and normalize these conversations.

Your mental health is just as important as your physical health, and while it's likely that you know and understand this, there's a chance you don't give your mental health the attention it needs.

In this book, you will learn the basics of DBT and CBT. You will also learn how to implement these skills in your day-to-day life. From regulating your emotions, to climbing out of the danger zone, and trying proven techniques to soothe yourself, this book will provide you with everything you need to get started on your journey to recovery. I hope that by reading this book, you will find the help that you need to live a content and fulfilling life.

This book is based on my personal experience and the tools that help me with mental illness. If you're struggling, please don't suffer in silence. Talk to somebody—a friend, a family member, or a therapist. There is help available, and you deserve to get the assistance you need. You are not alone.

It's normal to have emotions. It's normal to feel things, even if they make little sense initially. You are not crazy, and you are not alone. Emotions are a part of life, but sometimes they can feel overwhelming. When this happens, it's important to have

Introduction

tools and skills that you can use to cope with your emotions. This book will provide you with those tools. You are not defined by your mental illness or the challenges that you face. You are so much more than that, and I hope this book will help you see that.

No more allowing your emotions to determine your flow in life. It's time to take control and become the captain of your ship.

Chapter 1

The Cognitive-Behavioral Toolkit

You cannot always control what goes on outside, but you can always control what goes on inside.
—Wayne Dyer

Do you ever feel like you're fighting a battle against yourself? Are you struggling to control your thoughts? Do you feel like your beliefs are controlling your life? Have you noticed that if you're upset or angry, it's hard to see things clearly? Or that your behaviors are impacting your ability to achieve your goals? Maybe you can't seem to break out of a negative thought loop, or you keep getting derailed by old patterns of behavior. If you're ready to get a hold of your life and start feeling better, cognitive-behavioral therapy (CBT) can help. In this chapter, you will learn:

- What CBT is.

- How CBT can help you.

- The basic principles of CBT.

- The benefits and risks of CBT.

CBT Basics

Cognitive-behavioral therapy helps you change the way you think and act. CBT focuses on the relationship between the way you think and the way you behave. This therapy is based on the belief that your thoughts affect your emotions and your behaviors. Therefore, if you can change your thought process, the ripple effect changes your emotions and behaviors.

CBT is a problem-focused and goal-oriented therapy that helps people to identify and change negative thinking patterns and counterproductive behaviors. CBT can treat a wide variety of mental health conditions, including anxiety, depression, eating disorders, substance abuse, and more (American Psychological Association, 2017).

Here's an example:

Let's say you're thinking, *I'm a terrible person.* This is a thought that leads to negative emotions, such as low self-esteem, anxiety, and depression. It also leads to negative behaviors, such as not trying new things, not speaking up, and not taking risks.

Now, let's say you challenge that thought. You might say to yourself, *I am a good person who acts with the best intentions.* This is a thought that leads to positive emotions, such as high self-esteem, confidence, and happiness. It also leads to positive behaviors, such as trying new things, speaking up, and taking risks.

Or let's say you are feeling anxious. You might think, *I'm going to have a panic attack*. This thought can lead to the feeling of anxiety, which can then lead to the behavior of avoidance. However, by changing your thoughts and beliefs, you can change your emotions and actions.

As you can see, the thoughts you think have a direct impact on your life, but you have the power to change your thoughts.

Of course, changing your thoughts is easier said than done. But it's not impossible. With practice, you can learn to challenge your negative thoughts and replace them with positive ones. And when you do, you'll see a change in your life.

CBT is based on several principles. These principles are:

- Your thoughts affect your emotions and behaviors.
- You can change your thoughts.
- You can learn new ways of thinking.
- Practice makes perfect.

If you want to change your life, it's important to understand these principles and how CBT works.

How CBT Works

CBT works by teaching you different ways of thinking and behaving. CBT is typically done with a therapist, but there are also many self-help CBT resources available that can help you change your behaviors on your own. An assessment is usually the start of CBT. This is where you and your therapist will talk about your goals for therapy and what you hope to achieve.

Next, you and your therapist will work together to identify your negative thoughts and beliefs. Once you've identified your negative thoughts, you'll challenge them. You'll do this by looking at the evidence. For example, if you're thinking that you're not good enough, you'll look at all the evidence that shows that you are good enough. After you've questioned your negative thoughts, you'll replace them with positive ones.

The goals of CBT are to:

- Identify and change negative thinking patterns.

- Identify and change counterproductive behaviors.

- Improve mood.

- Reduce anxiety.

- Improve overall functioning.

CBT for Anxiety and Panic

If you're struggling with anxiety or panic, CBT can be very helpful. Since this technique can help you change your thoughts and behaviors, you can use it to help you challenge and reframe your anxieties. For instance, if you're anxious about going to work, CBT can help you challenge your thoughts about work.

Overall, your brain is hard-wired for survival, which is not a bad thing. It just means that you need to be aware of how your brain works and how it's affecting your life. Once you understand how your brain works, you can rewire it for happiness. If you're ready to make a change, consider CBT or DBT. These therapies can help you rewire your brain and change your life.

What Techniques Are Used in CBT?

Cognitive-behavioral therapy typically uses a variety of techniques, including

- Psychoeducation
- Cognitive restructuring
- Exposure therapy
- Behavioral experiments
- Skills training

These techniques help people label and reconstruct negative thinking patterns and counterproductive behaviors.

Modules of CBT

What Is Psychoeducation?

Psychoeducation is a technique that is used to educate people about mental health conditions. This type of education can help people to understand their condition and to learn about treatment options. For instance, you might learn about the different medications that are available to treat your condition. You might also learn about different therapy techniques, such as cognitive-behavioral therapy and dialectical behavior therapy (DBT).

What Is Exposure Therapy?

Exposure therapy is a type of cognitive-behavioral therapy that involves gradually exposing yourself to the things you fear. The goal of exposure therapy is to help you become less afraid of the things you avoid.

For example, if you are afraid of flying, exposure therapy might involve gradually exposing yourself to flying, first by watching videos or movies about flying, then by going to the airport and observing flights, and eventually by boarding a plane and taking a flight.

Exposure therapy is a very effective treatment for anxiety disorders. Studies have shown that exposure therapy can help people to reduce their fear, anxiety, and avoidance behavior.

Exposure Therapy Tactics:

Systematic desensitization: This technique helps people who have phobias or other anxiety disorders by slowly exposing them to the things that make them anxious or fearful in increments.

Flooding: People who suffer from PTSD or other anxiety disorders can use this technique to overcome their worries. It involves exposing yourself to the thing you fear all at once, instead of gradually.

Imaginal exposure: By imagining the thing you fear, instead of actually exposing yourself to it, you can practice overcoming challenges.

In-vivo exposure: This technique can assist people who have phobias or other anxiety disorders by exposing them to the situation or object they fear in real life, instead of in their imagination.

What Is Cognitive Restructuring?

Cognitive restructuring techniques help you identify and change negative thinking patterns. These techniques can help you learn how to think more realistically about the things you fear.

For example, if you are afraid of spiders, cognitive restructuring might involve identifying the thoughts and beliefs that contribute to that fear. Once you have identified these thoughts and beliefs, you can then challenge them and replace them with more realistic thoughts and beliefs.

Cognitive restructuring techniques are an important part of cognitive-behavioral therapy. These techniques can help you reduce your anxiety and improve your overall functioning.

Cognitive Restructuring Tactics:

Identifying negative thoughts: This technique helps you identify the negative thoughts or assumptions you make that contribute to your anxiety.

Challenging negative thoughts: Once you identify your negative thoughts, you use this technique to help you challenge and replace the negative thoughts that contribute to your anxiety.

Thought stopping: This cognitive technique involves you stopping the negative thoughts that enhance your anxiety the moment you notice them.

Positive visualization: You can use this technique to help you imagine positive outcomes.

What Are Behavioral Experiments?

Behavioral experiments assist you with testing out your beliefs concerning what you fear. For example, if you believe that flying is dangerous, you might want to test this belief by flying on a plane. Behavioral experiments can be helpful because they can help you see that your beliefs about the things you fear are often exaggerated and not based on reality.

What Are Skills Training?

Skills training is a type of cognitive-behavioral therapy that teaches you how to manage your symptoms. Skills training is an important part of cognitive-behavioral therapy. These skills can help you reduce your anxiety, manage your symptoms, and improve your overall functioning.

Skills Training Tactics:

Relaxation training: You can use relaxation training to soothe your body and mind. Examples of some practices include, but are not limited to, progressive muscle relaxation, deep breathing, and visualization.

Stress management: Learning to manage your stress is fundamental for this skill. For instance, you may practice proper time management skills, problem solving skills, or assertiveness training.

Assertiveness training: This skill helps you hone the art of communicating effectively and assertively, which has been known to reduce the anxiety you feel in social situations.

Cognitive-behavioral therapy is a highly effective treatment for anxiety disorders. If you are struggling with anxiety, CBT can help you identify and change the thinking patterns and behaviors that are contributing to your anxiety.

How Is CBT Different From Other Therapies?

Cognitive-behavioral therapy differs from other therapies in several ways. First, CBT is a short-term treatment that focuses on specific goals. Second, CBT is a problem-focused treatment that helps you understand your thought process and how it influences the behaviors that are contributing to your anxiety.

Benefits of CBT

Many mental health challenges have been shown to have great improvement with the help of CBT. The skills taught in CBT has been helpful in the treatment of a variety of anxiety disorders, including:

- Generalized anxiety disorder

- Panic disorder

- Phobias

- Social anxiety disorder (american psychological association, 2017).

CBT can help you reduce your anxiety, improve your functioning, and increase your quality of life.

Risks of CBT

CBT is a safe and productive treatment for anxiety disorders, but a few risks that may be associated with CBT include:

- Discomfort
  - CBT can involve some discomfort as you label, understand, or reframe the thoughts and actions that are contributing to your anxiety.

- Time commitment
  - CBT requires a time commitment. You will need to attend regular therapy sessions and do the work outside of therapy to see results.

- Cost
  - CBT can be costly, depending on the therapist you choose and your insurance coverage.

CBT and Individual Therapy

Cognitive behavioral therapy is typically provided in an individual therapy setting. In individual therapy, you will meet with a therapist regularly to work on your anxiety. In these sessions, you will learn about CBT and how to apply the techniques to your life. For instance, you may role-play situations that make you anxious so you can practice using CBT techniques.

CBT and Group Therapy

Cognitive behavioral therapy can also be provided in a group therapy setting. In group therapy, you will meet with a therapist and other people who are struggling with anxiety. This environment can be beneficial as you share your experiences and learn from others who are going through similar things.

CBT and Family Therapy

If you have a family member who is struggling with anxiety, consider family therapy. In family therapy, the whole family will meet with a therapist to work on the anxiety. In this environment, you and your family would learn about CBT and practice the techniques together.

How Long Does CBT Take?

Cognitive-behavioral therapy is a short-term treatment that typically lasts for 10-12 weeks. In some cases, CBT may be extended for longer periods of time.

What Happens After CBT?

After you finish cognitive-behavioral therapy, you might continue to see a therapist regularly. This can help you maintain the progress you have made and prevent anxiety from returning.

Key Takeaways

- A highly effective treatment for anxiety disorders and other mental health concerns is CBT. With the help of CBT, you can understand and reconstruct the thought processes and behaviors that are contributing to your anxiety.

- The techniques used in CBT are psychoeducation, cognitive restructuring, exposure therapy, behavioral experiments, and skills training.

- CBT is typically provided in an individual therapy setting, but it can also be done in a group or family setting. CBT is a short-term and problem-focused approach that helps you assess the way you think or behave and how it contributes to your anxiety.

- After completing CBT, you may choose to continue seeing a therapist to ensure you maintain the progress you have made and prevent returning to old behaviors.

Chapter 2

The Dialectical-Behavior Therapy Toolkit

Every time you are tempted to react in the same old way, ask if you want to be a prisoner of the past or a pioneer of the future.
—Deepak Chopra

Do you find yourself feeling stressed, overwhelmed, or unable to cope? Maybe you've been struggling to manage your emotions, deal with difficult situations, or cope with a major life change. If so, dialectical-behavior therapy skills may help. In the chapter, you will learn:

- About DBT and what it is.

- How DBT can help you.

- The four key areas of DBT.

- The benefits and risks of DBT.

Basics of DBT

Dialectical behavior therapy helps you change your thoughts and behaviors. It was derived from CBT and focuses on how your thoughts affect your emotions and your behaviors. If you can change your thoughts, then your emotions and behaviors will follow.

DBT's purpose is to help people understand and manage their emotions. DBT is a skills-based therapy that focuses on teaching you new skills to manage emotions and stress. Overall, these skills can help you reduce your anxiety, improve your relationships, and function better in everyday life.

Skills training can involve a variety of different techniques, including

- Relaxation training
- Stress management
- Assertiveness training
- Cognitive behavioral techniques

Skills training is critical for CBT techniques because you use them as a foundation to continue the rest of the principles

The principles of DBT are:

- Dialectics

- The principle of dialectics states that two opposite things can both be true. For example, you can be both happy and sad at the same time. This principle is helpful when you're struggling with emotional dysregulation because it helps you accept that you can have conflicting emotions. This philosophy is reflected in DBT through the balance of acceptance and change. DBT therapists work with their clients to accept themselves as they are while also working towards change.

- Dialectical thinking leads to creative solutions.

  - This principle is helpful when you're trying to solve a problem. It helps you consider both sides of the issue and find a creative solution.

- Change is possible.

  - The principle of change states that things can change. This is helpful when you're feeling stuck because when you believe that change is possible, you are more likely to make those adjustments in your life.

- Acceptance is necessary for change to occur.

  - The principle of acceptance states that you need to be honest with yourself about who you are before you can change. It helps you accept yourself as you are and believe that change is possible. Change has to become something that you want.

- Biosocial theory

  - Emotional dysregulation is caused by a combination of biological and social factors. Biological factors include things like genetics and neurobiology. Social factors include things like upbringing, environment, and culture.

History of DBT

Dialectical behavior therapy was developed in the 1980s by Dr. Marsha Linehan. She created this therapy technique to treat individuals with borderline personality disorder (BPD). People who suffer from BPD often experience intense emotions and have difficulty regulating their emotions. DBT helped people with BPD learn how to manage their emotions and cope with stress.

DBT skills training groups are typically led by two therapists, a co-leader and a group of 10-12 participants. The therapist and co-leader work together to teach the group members new skills. Skills training groups usually meet once a week for 2-3 hours.

What Is DBT Used For?

DBT can treat a variety of different mental health disorders. DBT has been an effective treatment for

- Borderline personality disorder

- Posttraumatic stress disorder

- Eating disorders

- Substance abuse disorders

- Depression

DBT can also treat anxiety disorders. DBT has be shown to improve

- Generalized anxiety disorder

- Social anxiety disorder

- Panic disorder (dialectical behavior therapy (dbt), n.d.).

DBT can be an effective treatment for anxiety because it teaches individuals new skills to manage their emotions and stress. DBT skills training can help you learn how to cope with your emotions healthily and manage stress effectively.

If you are struggling with anxiety, it is important to speak with a mental health professional to determine which therapy is right for you. However, combining the skills and techniques of each approach may be the most effective treatment for some individuals.

How DBT Works

DBT works by teaching you new ways of thinking and behaving. You would typically practice these skills with a therapist, but just like CBT, you can use self-help DBT books and resources available. DBT usually starts with an assessment, just like CBT.

First, you identify your negative thoughts and beliefs. Once you've identified your negative thoughts, you can challenge them, just like in CBT. DBT focuses on four areas: mindfulness, distress tolerance, interpersonal effectiveness, and emotion regulation.

Each of these areas will be addressed in therapy, and you'll learn new skills in each area. DBT takes time and effort, but it can be very effective. The more you practice, the better you'll get at it.

Mindfulness

Mindfulness is the focus on being present in the moment and accepting yourself as you are. This module will teach you how to be mindful of your thoughts, feelings, and behaviors. You will learn how to observe your thoughts and feelings without passing along your preconceived judgments. You will also learn how to be accepting of yourself, even if you are experiencing negative thoughts and emotions.

Mindfulness Tactics:

One-mindfully: By focusing on one task at a time, you would be practicing one-mindfully. For example, if you are eating, focus on the taste, smell, and texture of the food. If you are walking, focus on how your feet feel when they hit the ground.

Non-judgmentally: This technique involves observing your thoughts and feelings without judgment. Judgments can prevent you from seeing the situation clearly. Try to view your thoughts and feelings as if you were an outsider, without labeling them as good or bad.

Acceptance: Like CBT, this involves accepting yourself as you are and for who you are. You don't have to be happy with all of your thoughts and feelings. Acceptance means that you will experience and acknowledge them.

Interpersonal Effectiveness

The interpersonal effectiveness module will assist you in developing skills to manage relationships. You will learn how to communicate effectively, set boundaries, and manage conflict. You will also learn how to say "no" healthily.

Interpersonal Effectiveness Tactics:

Assertiveness: This technique involves communicating your needs in a clear and direct way. It is important to be assertive, not aggressive. Aggressive communication involves putting your needs above the needs of others. Assertive communication involves balancing your needs with the needs of others.

Empathy: Empathy involves understanding the feelings of other people. It is important to see things from another person's perspective, which can help you resolve conflicts.

Boundaries: Setting limits with the people in your life is important for healthy relationships, which is what this skill helps people learn to do.

Problem-solving: This technique involves using logical and creative thinking to solve problems. First, you identify the problem, generate potential solutions, and choose the best solution.

Distress Tolerance: The distress tolerance module will teach you how to cope with difficult situations healthily. You will learn how to manage distress and avoid destructive behaviors. You will also learn how to accept difficult situations and make positive changes.

Distress Tolerance Skills:

Radical acceptance: To put your acceptance skills to the test, you can use this method to practice moving forward in life, even when it's not ideal.

Mindfulness: By being present in the moment and practicing acceptance, you can build the tools you need to help you cope with difficult emotions.

Distraction: Redirecting your thoughts and energy away from the problem can help you cope with difficult emotions in the moment.

Self-soothing: This technique involves taking care of yourself through comfort. By self-soothing, you can cope with difficult emotions positively.

Improving the moment: You can use this skill to reframe your

```
         MFG Burgess Hill Service Station
                173 London Road
                   Burgess Hill
                   West Sussex
                    RH15 8LJ
                 Tel : 01444 226105


              Thu 08 Feb 2024 09:36:21


   Store 340 POS 1              Trans 178
   Op Name                        Manager


                       SALE


   VPower Unleaded                  £40.01
       Pump2: 25.02L @£1.599/L
   ─────────────────────────────────────────
   Total                            £40.01
   ─────────────────────────────────────────
   GBP                              £40.01
   ─────────────────────────────────────────


   Motor Fuel Ltd
   VAT No.                      123 4141 61
   VAT Rate     Ex.VAT      VAT     Inc.VAT
    20%          33.34     6.67       40.01
   Totals        33.34     6.67       40.01

   ─────────────────────────────────────────
                     Loyalty
   ─────────────────────────────────────────
```

```
          020003400100178080220242

                   Thank You
                Please Come Again
                 Drive Carefully
             Order Uber/Just Eat Online
                Costa Available Here

           Your Feedback is Important to us
           Please contact our Customer Care
                   on 01727 898890
                         or
            customercare@motorfuelgroup.com


                    Proudly Supporting
                   Man Cancer Support
```

thoughts to make a situation better. Used in the moment, you can cope with difficult emotions on the fly.

Emotion Regulation: The emotion regulation module will help you regulate your feelings healthily. You will learn how to identify and label your emotions. Then you can develop a healthy relationship with your emotions.

Emotion Regulation Skills:

Identifying emotions: To be able to regulate your emotions, you need to identify them. How are you feeling? Why?

Labeling emotions: Once you've identified them, name them. Are you feeling angry? Happy? Sad? Where does the emotion stem from?

Accepting emotions: After you've identified and labeled them, practice accepting them and letting them go.

Managing emotions: Emotions are normal, but they need to stay under control. This skill teaches you how you can manage your emotions properly.

Improving emotions: One way to manage your emotions is by practicing ways to improve them.

The goal of the modules is to help you develop skills that will reduce your anxiety and improve your overall functioning. DBT is a long-term treatment, and it may take several months to see the full benefits of therapy. However, you can expect to see some improvements after completing the skills training modules.

How Is DBT Different From Other Therapies?

DBT differs from other therapies because it focuses on the present moment and teaches skills to manage emotions. Other techniques may focus on the past or future, but DBT focuses on the here and now. DBT also teaches skills to manage emotions, whereas other therapies may focus on thoughts or behaviors.

What Are the Benefits of DBT?

The benefits of DBT include reduced anxiety, improved relationships, and better functioning in everyday life. DBT can also help people to develop a healthy relationship with their emotions.

What Are the Risks of DBT?

The risks of DBT are minimal. Some people may feel uncomfortable discussing their emotions in therapy. However, the therapist will work with you to ensure that you are comfortable with the level of disclosure.

DBT and Individual Therapy

DBT is typically done in individual therapy, but it can also be done in group therapy. In individual therapy, you will work one-on-one with a therapist to learn the skills of DBT. One-on-one may include phone calls, text messages, or online sessions. In these sessions, the therapist would teach you the skills of DBT and how to apply them to your life. You would also practice these skills with your therapist.

DBT and Group Therapy

DBT group therapy is typically done in addition to individual therapy. In group therapy, you will meet with other people who are also learning the skills of DBT. With the help of group therapy, you can learn the skills of DBT and practice them with other people. It can also be a supportive environment to share your experiences with anxiety and to get feedback from other people.

DBT and Family Therapy

DBT can also be done in family therapy. For these sessions, you would meet with your family members to learn the skills of DBT. Family therapy is a great way to learn the skills of DBT and to practice them with the people closest to you. This can also provide a supportive environment to share your experiences and communicate with others.

Key Takeaways

- DBT focuses on bringing your awareness to the present moment and teaches you skills so you can manage your emotions.

- The four key areas of DBT are: mindfulness, distress tolerance, emotion regulation, and interpersonal effectiveness.

- These tools help you to develop a healthy relationship with your emotions.

- You can practice DBT skills alone, in individual therapy, or group therapy.

- Reduced anxiety, improved relationships, and better functioning in life can result from using DBT techniques.

Chapter 3

The Dual Power of CBT and DBT

You don't have to control your thoughts; you just have to stop letting them control you.
—Dan Millman

Dealing with your emotions can be a difficult thing to do. It's easy to get caught up in an emotional tornado and feel like you're powerless to stop it. But you're not alone in this battle. That's where CBT and DBT come in. Using these therapy techniques together can help you take back control of your emotions and start living a more peaceful life. Although DBT was derived from CBT, they are two different therapies, with different focuses. Their practices are similar, but by using both therapies together, you can get the best of both worlds.

In this chapter you will learn:

- The differences between CBT and DBT.

- How using both these techniques can provide the most benefits.

- How to combine the modules of CBT and DBT.

Four Differences Between CBT and DBT

Although DBT was derived from CBT, there are a few key ways in which these two therapies differ.

1. CBT focuses on changing negative thoughts, while DBT focuses on changing behaviors.

2. CBT is more intellectual, while DBT is more action-oriented.

3. CBT focuses on the individual, while DBT focuses on the relationship between the individual and their environment.

4. CBT is more structured, while DBT is more flexible.

CBT Versus DBT Philosophies

Cognitive-behavioral therapy is a type of psychotherapy that focuses on identifying and changing negative thought patterns and behaviors. This technique is based on the philosophy that your thoughts control your emotions and your behavior. What this means is that if you can change the way you think, then the ripple effect continues, and you can change the way you feel and behave.

Dialectical behavior therapy is a type of psychotherapy that combines cognitive-behavioral therapy with Eastern mindful practices. However, this therapy is based on the opposite premise. DBT is based on the philosophy that your emotions control your thoughts and your behavior. Therefore, if you can change the way you feel, you can change the way you think and behave.

However, there are more significant differences between CBT and DBT. CBT concentrates on the problems that you experience and promotes goals that focus on helping the person identify negative thinking patterns and counterproductive behaviors so you can change them accordingly. CBT involves more intellectual, self-reflective work.

DBT is a skills-based therapy that focuses on teaching the individual new skills to manage emotions and stress. This therapy is focused on action and skills to prevent and de-escalate. DBT focuses on teaching individuals how to be present in the moment and accept themselves as they are. DBT also helps individuals to develop skills to manage relationships, cope with difficult situations, and regulate their emotions.

Both CBT and DBT are effective treatments for anxiety disorders. These therapies can help you change how you think, feel, or respond to your anxiety. However, each approach has its own unique features and the marriage of both can address the underlying issues while also gaining the awareness to use the more active tools when symptoms arise.

Both cognitive-behavioral therapy and dialectical behavior therapy are research-backed approaches that have been effective in treating anxiety disorders. Both CBT and DBT involve cognitive and behavioral techniques. When you combine these techniques together, you can create an individualized treatment approach that is tailored to your specific needs, which can be more effective for some.

DBT in Action: Dealing With Difficult Emotions

One of the most difficult things about living with anxiety is dealing with the negative emotions that come along with it. These emotions can be overwhelming and can make it difficult to cope with anxiety.

DBT can help you deal with these emotions in a more constructive way. DBT teaches skills that can help you regulate your emotions and to cope with difficult situations, which you can apply to your anxiety.

CBT in Action: Challenging Negative Thoughts

One of the most common symptoms of anxiety is negative

thinking. Negative thoughts can be incredibly overwhelming and can make it difficult to manage anxiety. CBT can help you challenge negative thoughts and to replace them with more positive ones. CBT teaches skills that can help you identify and change negative thought patterns. You can use these skills to manage anxiety and reduce the negative thoughts that come along with it.

The cognitive behavioral toolkit is a powerful tool for managing anxiety, helping you change the thoughts and emotions you have about your anxiety. CBT can help you challenge negative thoughts, while DBT can help you cope with negative emotions. These therapies can be incredibly useful for managing anxiety and for improving your overall mental health.

How Do I Know if CBT or DBT Is Better for Me?

CBT and DBT are both effective treatments for anxiety. However, each approach has its own unique benefits. For instance, CBT can help you identify and change thought patterns that affect your behavior. This technique uses skills to help you manage anxiety and reduce negative thinking. Some popular techniques are journaling and cognitive restructuring.

On the other hand, DBT can help you cope with difficult emotions. DBT uses mindfulness techniques to help you be more present in the moment. This approach can help you develop a more positive outlook on life.

The best way to know if CBT or DBT is better for you is to speak with a mental health professional. They can help you understand the benefits of each approach and create a treatment plan that meets your unique needs.

DBT Modules Versus CBT Modules

You can use several DBT modules to effectively treat anxiety. These modules teach skills that can help you manage your anxiety, cope with stress, and develop a more positive outlook on life.

DBT skill—mindfulness: Mindfulness is a core DBT skill that can manage anxiety. By learning how to focus your attention on the present moment and to accept your thoughts and feelings without judgment you can be happier.

Versus

CBT skill—relaxation techniques: Relaxation techniques can help you manage anxiety. By learning how to effectively relax your body and focus your attention, you can be mindful of the present moment.

DBT skill—distress tolerance: Distress tolerance teaches you how to cope with anxiety. You will learn how to effectively manage your emotions during times of distress.

Versus

CBT skill—stress management: You can manage anxiety by learning how to effectively cope with stressors and reframe your outlook on life.

DBT skill—emotion regulation: Emotion regulation can help you manage anxiety. This skill involves learning how to effectively manage your emotions and develop a more positive outlook on life.

Versus

CBT skill—cognitive restructuring: Cognitive restructuring can also help you manage anxiety. This skill involves learning how to challenge negative thoughts and to develop a more positive outlook on life.

DBT skill—interpersonal effectiveness: Interpersonal effectiveness is a DBT skill that can manage anxiety by learning how to effectively communicate your needs and to manage your relationships.

Versus

CBT skill—communication skills: By learning how to communicate your needs and manage your relationships in a healthy and productive way, you can combat your anxiety.

How to Combine CBT and DBT

CBT and DBT can be used together to create a comprehensive treatment plan for anxiety. This approach can be incredibly effective for managing anxiety disorders and improving your overall mental health. For instance, you might use CBT to challenge negative thoughts by practicing cognitive restructuring. Then, you might use DBT to cope with anxiety by learning mindfulness techniques. Or, you could combine the approaches where they have similar goals to complement each other. With the help of CBT and DBT, manage your uncertainty and live a more positive life.

Using CBT and DBT Modules Together

When used together, CBT and DBT modules can be an effective way to treat anxiety. This approach can help you learn a variety of skills that can manage your suffering so you can be more positive about life. For instance, you could combine the CBT skill of cognitive restructuring with the DBT skill of mindfulness. This would involve learning how to challenge negative thoughts and bring your focus to the present moment.

On the other hand, you could also combine the CBT skill of

communication with the DBT skill of interpersonal effectiveness. This would involve learning how to communicate in a productive way that would please others and benefit you as well.

You could also combine the CBT skill of stress management with the DBT skill of distress tolerance. This would involve learning how to effectively cope with stress and to manage your emotions during times of distress.

In general, the practices of DBT were derived from CBT practices. Therefore, it is not surprising that the two approaches share many similarities. While CBT focuses on changing negative thoughts and behaviors, DBT focuses on changing the way you react to your thoughts and emotions. This approach can be more effective in treating anxiety, as it can help you better manage your emotions and to develop a more positive outlook.

However, when combined, CBT and DBT can provide an even more comprehensive approach to treating anxiety. The dual approach can help you hone skills that can be used to manage your anxiety and reframe your beliefs.

Anxiety can be a debilitating condition that impacts every aspect of your life. If you suffer from anxiety, you may experience a range of symptoms, including difficulty concentrating, feeling irritable or on edge, feeling restless or keyed up, sweating, trembling, and shortness of breath. Anxiety can also lead to avoidance behaviors, such as avoiding social situations or places that make you feel anxious.

Combining Mindful Meditation and CBT Skills

To create a treatment plan for anxiety, you can combine CBT and mindfulness meditation. These approaches can help you control your anxiety and improve your overall mental health. You could challenge negative thoughts by practicing cognitive restructuring. Then, you might use mindfulness meditation as a coping mechanism for anxiety.

Combining Distress Tolerance and CBT Skills

Combine CBT and distress tolerance to create a comprehensive treatment plan for anxiety. You can use these approaches to manage anxiety, other emotions, and improve your mental health as well. You could practice cognitive restructuring journaling and then, you might use distress tolerance to cope with anxiety by incorporating mindful activities or by participating in exposure therapy.

Combining Emotion Regulation and CBT Skills

Together, CBT and emotion regulation can also be an effective treatment plan for anxiety. You can also use this effective approach for managing anxiety and improving your overall mental health. You could start by challenging your negative thoughts by practicing cognitive restructuring. Then, you might use emotion regulation to cope with anxiety by learning how to effectively manage your emotions.

Combining Interpersonal Effectiveness and CBT Skills

You can use CBT skills and interpersonal effectiveness to create a treatment plan for anxiety. You could use CBT to challenge negative thoughts using cognitive restructuring or by practicing communication skills. Then, you might use interpersonal effectiveness to cope with anxiety by focusing on managing your relationships.

Pros and Cons of Combining CBT and DBT

There are both advantages and disadvantages to using CBT and DBT together to treat anxiety. Some benefits of this approach include:

- You can learn a variety of skills to manage anxiety.

- You can tailor the treatment plan to your specific needs.

- You can choose which skills you want to focus on.

- You might find it easier to stick with treatment if you're using both approaches.

- You can get support from a therapist who is trained in both CBT and DBT.

- You might have more success with treatment if you use

both approaches.

Some drawbacks of this approach include:

- You may need to see a therapist who is trained in both therapy practices, which may be difficult to find.
- You may need to take part in more than one therapy session per week.
- You may need to take medication to manage your anxiety.
- You may feel overwhelmed by the number of skills you need to learn.

If you decide to use CBT and DBT to treat your anxiety, it is important to work with a therapist who is trained in both approaches. This will ensure that you are getting the most out of your therapy sessions. It is also important to be patient and to remember that it may take some time to learn all the skills you need to manage your anxiety. But, with the help of a qualified therapist, you can develop an effective treatment plan that will work for you.

CBT and DBT for Emotional Sensitivity

If you're struggling with emotional sensitivity, you might benefit from cognitive-behavioral therapy or dialectical behavioral therapy. CBT focuses on changing the way you think about your emotions. For example, if you're anxious about an upcoming event, CBT can help you reframe your thinking. Instead of thinking, *I'm going to fail*, you might start thinking, *I'm going to do my best*.

DBT prompts you to change the way you respond to your emotions. For example, if you're feeling overwhelmed by sadness, DBT can help you develop healthy coping strategies. You might learn how to take breaks, set boundaries, or talk to a therapist about your emotions. CBT and DBT can help you develop healthy coping strategies to combat emotional sensitivity. Seek professional help to find a therapist who can help you.

CBT and DBT for Emotional Distress

If you're struggling with emotional distress, CBT and DBT can assist you with developing healthy coping strategies. Some strategies include:

- Learning how to identify and challenge negative thoughts.

- Developing healthy coping mechanisms.

- Identifying and challenging negative thoughts.

- Identifying the thought.

- Labeling the emotion you're feeling.

- Challenging the thought.

- Replacing the thought with a more realistic one.

Example:

Negative thought: *I can't do this. I'm going to fail.*

Emotion: fear

Evidence: I don't have any evidence that I'm going to fail. I can't predict the future.

Key Takeaways

- CBT and DBT are two types of therapy that can help you manage your emotions.

- CBT promotes and assists the change in the way you think about your emotions and focuses on challenging thought distortions to more realistic ones.

- DBT prompts a change in how you respond to your feelings and focuses on mindfulness and acceptance.

- DBT was derived from CBT but has a more Eastern philosophical orientation.

- CBT and DBT can teach you healthy coping techniques to deal with emotional sensitivity, distress, or anxiety.

Chapter 4

Why Is Your Brain Against You?

Anxiety was born in the very same moment as mankind. And since we will never be able to master it, we will have to learn to live with it—just as we have learned to live with storms.
—Paulo Coelho

Does it seem like your brain is against you? Does life seem as if all hope has disappeared from within, only for a glimmering light to appear on top of an anxious pile of stressors, which stimulates worry about how much control you really have over your life?

Perhaps you want to be happy, but your brain is always filled with anxious thoughts. Maybe you want to be productive, but your brain keeps procrastinating, and when you try to change your life, it feels like your brain is fighting you every step of the way. It feels sabotaging and tiring, doesn't it?

If this sounds familiar, don't worry, you're not alone. In fact, this is a very common experience. Your brain is wired to resist change, but that doesn't mean it's against you. In fact, the reason your brain feels like this all stems from its programming and not because of any nefarious intentions on behalf of yours or anyone else's part!

This may seem strange, but it makes perfect sense when you understand how the brain works. The brain is a really smart organ, but sometimes it goes too far in protecting us from danger, which it does by maintaining the status quo.

The problem comes into play when you want to change aspects of yourself for the better. For example, quitting smoking is good for your health, but it's also a big change and your brain doesn't like change.

Your brain has evolved to protect you from danger, and sometimes it goes overboard. When you're anxious or panicking, it's because your brain mistakenly thinks that there's something dangerous happening when there isn't.

Survival Triumphs Happiness

Your brain is wired to prioritize survival over happiness. This may seem like a strange thing to say, but it's true. The reason for this is that, from an evolutionary perspective, it's more important to survive than to be happy. Happiness is a luxury that your ancestors, meaning the cavemen, couldn't afford.

The Caveman Brain

The brain is an amazing organ, and it's come a long way since the days of the cavemen, but it's important to understand that the brain is still wired for survival. This means that, even though you're not in danger of being eaten by a saber-toothed tiger, your brain still thinks you are, which can lead to a lot of anxiety and stress.

In order to survive, the cave dweller brain needed to be aware of danger lurking in any corner. They needed to work in groups and look out for the people in their inner circle. Since they worked in groups, they needed to pull their weight, otherwise they would be exiled. Cavemen needed to have the best weapons to hunt and protect their families. These wants and needs of the cave dwellers are still deeply ingrained in you. However, what changed from then to now are your circumstances or surroundings and not your brain.

The chances of you encountering a wild animal that will attack you are slim to none. You don't need to work in groups to protect yourself and your family, and you definitely don't need the best weapons to hunt. However, your brain hasn't caught up to these changes just yet.

Therefore, you still feel anxiety and stress. Your brain still has those concerns, but applies it in different ways. For instance, an animal is unlikely to put you in danger, so what can be dangerous is not having a job or not being able to provide for your family. Sometimes your brain goes to an extreme and you might worry about things that are very unlikely to happen, such as winning the lottery or being in a social environment. The threat of survival isn't as strong, so your fears get projected onto

circumstances more relatable to the times you're in.

Although you don't have to work in groups to survive, that's another evolutionary tactic that has stayed with you. Instead, you focus on what others may think of how or how you can impress the people you know because, in the caveman days, if you couldn't prove to be useful, you would be exiled. That would mean certain death.

However, you live in a time and age where, thanks to the internet, you have access to almost everyone and anything. Instead of focusing on your tight-knit group, you have a global community at your fingertips. The need to belong is still deeply ingrained in you, but it manifests itself in different ways.

Cave dwellers were also concerned with having the best weapons to hunt. Now, you're not looking for the best weapons, but the best tools. You want to have the best education so you can get the best job. You want to have the best clothes so you can make a good impression. You want to have the best car so you can show off your success. These things result from the caveman brain hardwired for survival.

The bottom line is that your brain is still wired for the survival tactics the cavemen needed many centuries ago, which is not a bad thing. By understanding how your brain works and why it affects your life, you can rewire it for happiness.

Brains Sabotage the Present Moment

Have you ever noticed how your mind is always thinking about the future or dwelling on the past? It's like your brain is trying to protect you from the present moment, and in some ways, it is. The present moment can be uncomfortable, especially if you're not used to being present. If you're used to living in your head, then the present moment can feel like a foreign place.

When your brain is not activated with a task, it will often try to find something to do, and sometimes, that something is worrying. Worry is the brain's way of protecting you from future danger. It's a normal part of human nature, but when you get stuck in a cycle of worry, it can be very hard to break free.

If you are someone who worries a lot, you might have noticed how your mind always seems to jump ahead to the future. Your brain is protecting you from what it thinks might happen, even though there's no evidence that anything bad will actually happen.

On the opposite side of the spectrum, you might notice that your brain switches to the past. Your brain might ruminate on the past as a way of trying to protect yourself from making the same mistakes again. Both reactions are normal, but equally frustrating.

However, it's important to understand that your brain is just doing its job. It's trying to protect you from danger. However, you can teach your brain to be more present and when you're more present, you're less likely to worry about the future.

A popular technique to remain focused on the present is to practice mindfulness. Mindfulness is a skill that teaches you to be aware of the present moment on purpose without judging or reacting. The keywords for this skill are "on purpose" because if you're not making a conscious intention to focus on the present, your brain turns to autopilot.

When your brain turns to autopilot, it means that your thoughts are on autopilot as well. That's when your mind wanders, and you get caught in the whirlwind of emotions and thoughts. However, if you intentionally focus on the present moment, you can program your brain to be more present.

When you're mindful, you're not only aware of what's going on around you, but you're also aware of your thoughts and feelings. You're able to observe them without reacting to them. This might sound easy, but it's actually quite difficult. That's because your thoughts and feelings are powerful. They can easily take over and hijack your attention. The good news is that the more you practice mindfulness, the easier it becomes.

Many mindful practices are available for your use, from walking meditations to mindful eating techniques. Listed below are two exercises to help you practice being more mindful.

Mindful Eating Exercise

This is an exercise to help you be more mindful of your eating habits. It can be done alone or with a partner.

1. Sit down in a comfortable position and take a few deep breaths.

2. Close your eyes and begin to focus on your breath.

3. Once you have focused on your breath, begin to pay attention to the sensations in your body.

4. Notice any hunger or thirst you may be feeling.

5. Once you have identified any hunger or thirst, begin to focus on the taste, smell, and texture of the food or drink you are consuming.

6. Pay attention to how your body feels after you have eaten or drunk.

7. Repeat this exercise each time you eat or drink throughout the day.

8. At the end of the day, reflect on your experience with this exercise. What were some things you noticed about your eating habits you were previously unaware of? What challenges did you face with this exercise? How can you overcome these challenges in the future?

Mindful Body Scan Exercise

You can use this exercise to be more mindful of your body and can be done alone or with a partner.

1. Sit or lie down comfortably and take a few deep breaths.

2. Shut your eyes and concentrate on your breath.

3. Once you're aware of your breathing pattern, begin to scan your body starting with your feet by focusing on your toes.

4. Notice any sensations you are feeling in your feet. Wiggle your toes, if you'd like.

5. Once you have focused on your feet, move up to your legs and notice any sensations you are feeling in your legs.

6. Continue to move up your body, noticing any sensations you are feeling in each area until you reach your head.

7. Once you have reached your head, pay attention to any thoughts or emotions you are experiencing.

8. After you have completed the body scan, take a few deep breaths and reflect on your experience. What were some things you noticed about your body that you were previously unaware of? What challenges did you face with this exercise and how can you overcome them the next time?

How To Rewire Your Brain

The good news is that you can rewire your brain for happiness, and it all starts with understanding how your brain works. Your brain is always looking for patterns. This is how it learned to survive in the days of the cavemen. If you saw a saber-toothed tiger, you would know that it is a danger. It would see a group of people and learn that this is a safe place. It would see a weapon and know that it can be used for hunting.

Now, your brain is still looking for patterns, but the patterns have changed. However, you can change the patterns that your brain is looking for. The first step is to notice your thoughts. This is easier said than done because your thoughts are so ingrained in yourself that you don't even realize you're thinking about them, but if you pay attention, you'll notice the patterns in your thoughts.

Once you become aware of your thoughts, you can challenge them. This is where CBT or DBT skills come in handy. If you're not familiar with CBT or DBT, they stand for Cognitive-Behavioral Therapy and Dialectical Behavior Therapy, respectively. Both therapies are formed from the belief that your thoughts, your emotions, and your behaviors are all interconnected, which means they affect each other like a domino effect. If you can change your thoughts, then you can change the ripple effect that is your emotions and behaviors.

Here's an example:

Let's say you're thinking, *I'm not good enough*. This thought can cultivate negative emotions and poor behaviors or self-medicating to make yourself feel better.

Now, let's say you challenge that thought. You might say to yourself, *I am good enough*. This can cultivate positive emotions. It can also promote positive behaviors, like being more assertive in relationships or facing your fears.

Although change can be arduous, it's not impossible. With practice, you can learn to accomplish this quicker and see vast improvements in your life.

Neuroplasticity

You may have heard of the term "neuroplasticity." Neuroplasticity is the ability of the brain to change and adapt, which is something everybody can do. Neuroplasticity used to be thought of as something that only happened in children. However, it's been proven that neuroplasticity occurs throughout your life. It's a prime reason you can learn new skills and change your behavior. Having neuroplasticity means that you can change your brain, which is good news for those of you who want to rewire your brain for happiness.

What Does This Mean For Me?

If you're reading this, chances are you're not happy with the way your life is going. Maybe you're struggling with anxiety, depression, or some other issue and you're looking for a way to make a change. The good news is that you can make significant changes by understanding how your brain processes information and using CBT or DBT skills to rewire your brain.

Chapter 5

The Root of Anxiety, Worry, and Panic

Anxiety is a thin stream of fear trickling through the mind. If encouraged, it cuts a channel into which all other thoughts are drained.
—Arthur Somers Roche

Have you experienced tremendous worry? Anxiety? Panic? All the above? Do you know what triggered those feelings? Do you know what was going on in your mind during those times? It can feel like the ground is shaking beneath your feet. You may feel like you are going crazy. Your heart races. You can't think straight. You may even feel like you are going to die. If so, you are not alone. Millions of people experience these feelings every day. In this chapter, you will learn:

- What anxiety is.

- Why you may worry or panic.

- How to overcome anxiety.

For worry, anxiety, and panic, it is important to understand the root of these emotions in order to better control them. The root of worry, anxiety, and panic is often found in your thought patterns and beliefs. Your thoughts can be incredibly powerful and can cause you to feel a wide range of emotions from happiness to sadness to fear. If you worry about something that is not real, or if you believe that something bad is going to happen, then you will probably feel anxious or even panicked.

What Is Anxiety?

Anxiety is a feeling of worry, nervousness, or unease. It is a normal human emotion that we experience when we face something stressful. Everyone experiences anxiety in their life. For most people, anxiety is short-lived and goes away once the stressful situation has passed. However, for some people, anxiety can become chronic and last for long periods of time.

What Is the Difference Between Anxiety and Worry?

Anxiety and worry are often used interchangeably, but they are actually two different things. Worry is a thought process that anxious people use to control their fear. It is a type of negative thinking that creates more anxiety. Anxiety, on the other hand, is an emotion that you feel in response to a perceived threat. It is the body's natural way of preparing us to deal with danger.

What Is the Difference Between Anxiety and Panic?

Panic is a type of anxiety that is characterized by sudden and intense fear. Panic attacks are a physical manifestation of this fear and can include symptoms such as rapid heart rate, shortness of breath, and dizziness. These attacks can be very frightening and may feel like you are having a heart attack or dying.

What Are the Different Anxiety Disorders?

A variety of anxiety disorders exist, and each has its own set of symptoms. The most common types of anxiety disorders are:

- Generalized anxiety disorder (GAD)
- Social anxiety disorder (SAD)
- Panic disorder (PD)
- Agoraphobia
- Specific phobias

What Are the Symptoms of Anxiety?

Anxiety can come in many forms, and the symptoms you experience can vary depending on the type of disorder. However, some common symptoms of anxiety include:

- Feeling restless or on edge
- Feeling overwhelmed or like you can't cope
- Having difficulty concentrating
- Feeling irritable
- Having muscle tension
- Trouble sleeping
- Sweating
- Heart palpitations
- Shortness of breath
- Nausea
- Dizziness

If you are experiencing any of these symptoms, it is important to seek professional help.

How Is Anxiety Treated?

Anxiety can be an overwhelming feeling, but luckily, many treatment options are available for anxiety. The most common treatments are:

- Therapy
- Medication
- Exercise
- Relaxation techniques

It is important to find a treatment that works for you. Some people may need to try a few different treatments before they find one that is effective because each person has unique features that affect their response to treatments.

What Causes Anxiety?

There is no one cause of anxiety. It is thought to be caused by a combination of genetic and environmental factors. Some people may experience anxiety more than others due to their genes, while others may develop anxiety in response to a traumatic event. Some environmental factors that can contribute to anxiety include:

- Stress

- Family conflict
- Financial problems
- Work pressure
- Social isolation

The Hidden Root of Anxiety

Although several factors can contribute to anxiety, such as stress, family conflict, and financial problems, there is a hidden root of anxiety that is often overlooked: fear.

Much like anxiety, you feel fear when your mind or body believes there is a threat. It is the body's natural way of preparing you to deal with danger. When you face a situation that makes you feel afraid, your body triggers the fight-or-flight response. This is a survival mechanism that dates back to your ancestors. The fight-or-flight response is an instinct that kicks in when you are in danger. It helps you to either fight the threat or run away from it.

In today's world, you rarely face life-threatening situations. However, your fight-or-flight response can still be triggered by things like public speaking, examinations, and interviews. When this happens, you may experience symptoms of anxiety, such as having a panic attack.

The key to overcoming anxiety is to face your fears. This may sound easier said than done, but it is possible when you develop courage. When you face your fears, you are teaching your brain that there is nothing to be afraid of. This will help to rewire your brain and reduce your anxiety.

Developing Courage

Imagine the scariest thing you've ever done. Chances are it wasn't doing something without fear, but rather facing your fears and overcoming them to do what had to be done anyway, even if that meant going into an unknown space where there were potential dangers waiting for you.

When involved in a situation that makes you anxious and afraid, it's natural to want nothing more than to curl up in the fetal position. However, you can still choose not only to face your fears, but also to do something about them, no matter how scared you feel at first. Fear is a normal human emotion. It's what drives you to hide from your fears instead of facing them and doing something about those things that scare you most in life, like going after your dreams or taking risks (even if it means making mistakes). Courage, importantly, isn't the absence of fear—it's feeling scared, but still choosing to show up for yourself today.

Here are some tips for developing courage:

- Acknowledge your fear
    - The first step is to acknowledge that you are feeling afraid. Accepting your fear will help you deal with it in a more positive way.

- Breathe

  - Take some deep breaths and focus on your breathing. This will help to calm your nervous system and reduce the symptoms of anxiety.

- Visualize success

  - See yourself succeeding when you are afraid of. Visualizing yourself being successful will help to boost your confidence and reduce your anxiety.

- Take action

  - Once you have visualized yourself being successful, it is time to take action. This may mean facing your fear head-on or taking small steps towards your goal.

- Reward yourself

  - After you have taken action, reward yourself for your courage. This will help to reinforce the positive behavior and make it more likely that you will do it again in the future.

Facing your fears can be a scary experience, but it is an essential part of overcoming anxiety. By facing your fears, you will realize there's nothing to be afraid of. Then you can rewire your brain and reduce your anxiety by cultivating more positive thoughts regarding your fears.

What Are Some Tips for Managing Anxiety?

Managing your anxiety is not an effortless task. People living with anxiety often feel isolated, which leads them to feelings of guilt for wanting more attention than necessary. It's important to find the right balance between doing what you need and coping with stressors in life as best we can! Here are some tips for managing or reducing feelings of fear, worry, and dread.

Some tips include:

- Identify your triggers

  - What are the things that make your anxiety worse? Once you know what your triggers are, you can try to avoid them or be prepared for them.

- Challenge your negative thoughts

  - When you're feeling anxious, your mind may tell you "facts" that are not true. For example, you may tell yourself that you are going to fail or that everyone is judging you. It is important to challenge these negative thoughts and remind yourself that they are not true.

- Breathe

  - When you're feeling anxious, your breathing may become shallow and rapid. This can make your anxiety worse. Try to take deep, slow breaths to calm yourself down.

- Exercise

    - Exercise can help to reduce stress and improve your mood. It is also a great way to get rid of excess energy that can make your anxiety worse.

- Relax

    - Try relaxation techniques such as yoga, meditation, and deep breathing, all of which can help to reduce anxiety.

- Talk to someone

    - Talking to a friend, family member, therapist, or doctor can help you feel better and may help you find solutions to your problems.

Anxiety is a treatable condition, and with the right treatment, you can live a happy and healthy life.

Identifying the Root of Your Anxiety

Anxiety can be caused by many things. It is important to identify the root of your anxiety so that you can address it. Some common causes of anxiety include:

- Genetic factors

    - Anxiety can be passed down from your parents. If

someone in your family has anxiety, you are more likely to experience it as well.

- Life experiences

    o   Traumatic or stressful life experiences can trigger anxiety.

- Medical conditions

    o   Some medical conditions can cause anxiety. For example, an overactive thyroid gland can cause anxiety.

- Substance abuse

    o   Using drugs or alcohol can cause anxiety.

- Withdrawals

    o   Withdrawing from drugs or alcohol can also cause anxiety.

A therapist or counselor can help you identify the cause of your anxiety and develop a treatment plan. Below is a "worry" exercise where you can identify your worries and determine how accurate your perception is.

Worry Exercise: What Can Versus What Will Happen

When you're worried about a situation, it's easy to resort to the worst possible thoughts. However, these thoughts are often extreme and may not happen. Playing the "what if" game doesn't mean it'll actually happen. Below are prompts to help you determine how accurate your worry is and how to lessen the anxiety that comes with the unknown.

Scenario: What are you worried about?

Scenario: What are you worried about?

Instead of thinking about what *could* happen, think about what *will* most likely happen. Focusing on infinite possibilities can cause you to worry more. When you find yourself spiraling into the "what ifs" listed below are some questions you can ask yourself.

What are signs that your fears will *not* come true?

What will likely happen if your fears don't come true?

If the worst possible outcome *does* happen, how can you handle it? What will the end outcome be? Will you eventually overcome these challenges and be ok?

Reflection: After answering the above questions, have your worries changed?

Keep a Kind and Open-Minded Mindset

When you're ready to identify the root of your anxiety, keep a nice and open-minded mindset. Don't get too caught up in what you think is causing your anxiety. Instead, be open to exploring all possibilities. It is also important to be patient. It may take some time to figure out the root of your anxiety, but with patience and perseverance, you will eventually find the answer.

A popular acronym to help you with understanding your emotions is ACCEPTS. According to Therapistaid, ACCEPTS stands for activities, contributing, comparisons, emotions, pushing away, thoughts, and sensations.

Activities: Doing activities you enjoy can improve your mood by releasing endorphins. When you are feeling down, try to do something that you enjoy or that makes you feel good.

Contributing: Contributing to something can make you feel good about yourself and help take your mind off of your own problems. Help others and you will probably find that your mood improves as well.

Comparisons: Although comparisons can sometimes make you feel worse, if you do it appropriately, you can put yourself and the situation into perspective. Try comparing the situation to something you've experienced that was worse. How does it compare?

Emotions: Emotions are normal and natural, but can be overwhelming. To combat a negative emotion, try to create a new emotion that would override the one you're feeling.

Pushing away: You can avoid certain thoughts or situations by "pushing it away." Use a technique like visualization or do an activity you enjoy to direct your mind away from the challenges that are influencing you.

Thoughts: When you indulge in your thoughts, your body reacts, and emotions follow along. If you're experiencing negative thoughts, push them away. Thoughts are just thoughts. They don't have to control you; in fact, they come and go without you even realizing it. You can either acknowledge the thought and then let it go or reframe your thoughts to be more neutral or positive rather than focusing on the negatives.

Sensations: By altering your physical state in a healthy way, you can change your emotions.

Below is an ACCEPTS worksheet to help you put these skills to use.

ACCEPTS Worksheet

What situation is concerning you? What emotion do you want to overcome?

Activities: Which activities can you engage in that will require focus so you can distract yourself from the emotion?

Contribute: What activities can you do that focus on others?

Comparison: When else have you experienced a distressing emotion? How did you overcome it and how does it compare to what you're experiencing now?

Emotions: What new emotion can you cultivate and how?

Pushing away: How can you avoid the thoughts or situation that is causing you to experience this negative emotion?

Thoughts: What mental strategies can you use to reframe your thoughts?

Sensations: Which safe but effective ways can you use to change your physical state? (holding an ice cube, taking a cold shower, eating spicy food, etc.)

Befriend Your Anxiety

Once you have identified the root of your anxiety, it is time to befriend your anxiety. This may sound strange, but it is important to remember that anxiety is just a feeling. It is not who you are. Anxiety is something that you have, not something that you are.

It is also important to remember that anxiety is normal. Everyone experiences anxiety in their life. It is a natural response to stress and danger. Anxiety is only a problem when it interferes with your life.

So how do you befriend your anxiety? Here are some tips:

- Accept your anxiety

  - The first step is to accept that you have anxiety. This may be difficult, but remember that anxiety is normal and everyone experiences it in their life.

- Talk to your anxiety

  - Once you have accepted your anxiety, it is time to talk to it. This may sound strange, but it's helpful to think of your anxiety as a separate entity. When you're feeling anxious, talk to your anxiety and ask it what it wants.

- Listen to your anxiety

  - After you have talked to your anxiety, it is time to listen to it. What is your anxiety trying to tell you? Is it trying to protect you from something? Is it trying to warn you about something?

- Thank your anxiety

    - Once you have listened to your anxiety, it is time to thank it. Thank your anxiety for trying to protect you. Thank it for its warning. And then let it go.

- Challenge your anxiety:

    - Once you have accepted, talked to, listened to, and thanked your anxiety, it is time to challenge it. When you're feeling anxious, ask yourself if there is really anything to be anxious about. Often, we are anxious about things that are not actually dangerous.

- Breathe

    - When you're feeling anxious, it is important to remember to breathe. Anxiety can cause us to take shallow breaths, which can make us feel more anxious. So when you're feeling anxious, take a few deep breaths and relax.

- Get acquainted with your anxiety

    - Getting acquainted with your anxiety means determining your triggers. Where and when does anxiety impact you? What are the circumstances that lead to anxiety? Once you have identified your triggers, you can avoid them or be prepared for them. It also helps to record the symptoms of your experience and for how long.

- List your fears
  - Remember, the most overlooked cause of anxiety is fear. So, it's important to inspect your fears. What are you afraid of? Are you afraid of failure? Of success? Of being alone? Of being rejected? Of being hurt?

- Determine the patterns
  - Look for patterns in your anxiety. Do you tend to be more anxious at certain times of the day? Or in certain situations? Once you have identified the patterns, you can change them.

- Choose your battles
  - Not all anxiety is terrible. In fact, some anxiety can be helpful. For example, anxiety can motivate us to take action and change our lives. But not all anxiety is helpful. And sometimes, we need to choose our battles.

- Confront your fears
  - Confronting your fears may sound daunting, but it is important to remember that courage is not the absence of fear, but the ability to face your fears.

THINC MED Acronym

Sometimes our anxiety has to do more with our physical health than our mental health. A routine checkup might help you identify any physical health concerns that might cause or contribute to your anxiety. The THINC MED acronym can help you and your doctor look for specific problems that might cause your anxiety. According to Therapistaid, THINC MED stands for:

Tumors: Not only can tumors add to anxiety depending on their location or intensity, but they can also cause personality changes or hallucinations. It is important to rule out any physical health concerns.

Hormones: Hormonal imbalances can cause anxiety. This is especially true for women who are pregnant or going through menopause.

Infectious diseases: Some infectious diseases can cause anxiety. For example, Lyme disease can cause anxiety and panic attacks.

Nutritional deficiencies: Deficiencies in certain vitamins and minerals can cause anxiety. For example, a lack of magnesium can cause anxiety.

Central nervous system: disorders of the central nervous system can cause anxiety. For example, Alzheimer's disease can cause anxiety.

Miscellaneous: Several other physical health concerns can cause anxiety. For example, sleep apnea, chronic migraines, or food allergies can cause anxiety.

Electrolyte abnormalities and environmental toxins: Electrolyte abnormalities and environmental toxins can also cause anxiety. For example, lead poisoning can cause anxiety.

Drugs: Aside from recreational drugs, some drugs or medications can cause anxiety. For example, withdrawal from alcohol or caffeine can cause anxiety. Even over-the-counter medications can cause anxiety. So, it is important to talk to your doctor about any medications you are taking.

Key Takeaways

- Anxiety is a normal and necessary emotion that helps us cope with stress, but when anxiety becomes excessive, it can be debilitating.

- The hidden root of anxiety is often fear. So, it's important to identify your fears and confront them.

- To manage your anxiety, you can:
    - Identify your triggers.
    - List your fears.

- Determine the patterns.
- Confront your fears.
- Choose your battles.

● If you are struggling with anxiety, consider talking to your doctor. They can perform an exam to rule out physical health concerns that might contribute to your anxiety.

Chapter 6

Emotional Numbness

It's not stress that kills us, it is our reaction to it.
—Hans Selye

Have you ever felt disconnected from your emotions, like you can't feel anything, or that nothing matters? For instance, you might see a movie that's supposed to be sad, but you feel nothing, or someone close to you dies, and you don't feel as sad as you think you should. This disconnection from your emotions is called emotional numbness. Emotional numbness is a common symptom of post-traumatic stress disorder (PTSD) and can be extremely debilitating. In this chapter, you will learn about:

- What emotional numbness is.

- How to identify emotional numbness.

- The causes of emotional numbness.

- How to overcome emotional numbness.

What Is Emotional Numbness?

Emotional numbness is a condition where you feel disconnected from your emotions. You may not sense anything at all, or even know what's going on inside of yourself and around you emotionally—it could just seem like everything has lost its meaning for a while there.

You may feel you can't feel anything or that your emotions are blunted. You may also feel you're in a fog or that you're disconnected from yourself and the world around you. You may feel numb, empty, or dead inside. If you're feeling emotionally numb, it's important to understand that this is a common reaction to trauma and isn't something you should feel ashamed of.

Being emotionally numb is a way of coping with what's happened and is actually helping you to protect yourself in the short-term. In the long-term, though, it's important to find other ways of managing your emotions so that you can eventually start to feel them again.

Symptoms of Emotional Numbness

The symptoms of emotional numbness can vary from person to person. However, some signs and symptoms that many people experience are more common.

Some common symptoms of emotional numbness include:

- Feeling disconnected from your emotions
- Feeling like you can't feel anything
- Feeling like your emotions are blunted
- Feeling like you're in a fog
- Feeling disconnected from yourself and the world around you
- Having trouble concentrating
- Feeling detached from your body
- Feeling like you're watching your life from outside of your body
- Numbing yourself with alcohol or drugs
- Engaging in risky or self-destructive behaviors

If you're experiencing any of these symptoms, it's important to reach out for help.

Causes of Emotional Numbness

A few different theories are believed to contribute to emotional numbness. One theory is that it's a defense mechanism. When someone experiences a traumatic event, they might numb their emotions to cope. This can help them feel less pain and prevent them from reliving the trauma repeatedly. Another theory is that emotional numbness is a symptom of dissociation.

Dissociation is when a person feels disconnected from their body or their surroundings. They might feel like they're watching themselves from outside of their body, or like they're in a dream. Dissociation can be a way to cope with trauma, or it can be a symptom of another mental health condition, such as posttraumatic stress disorder. If you're feeling emotionally numb, it's important to talk to a mental health professional. A professional can guide you to understand why you're feeling this way and provide you with tools to deal with it.

Some common causes of emotional numbness include:

Stress: If you're constantly under stress, your emotions may start to feel blunted. Stress activates the fight-or-flight response and when this happens, your body produces cortisol. Cortisol numbs your emotions and makes it difficult to feel anything.

Anxiety: When you're anxious, your body goes into fight-or-flight mode. This causes your body to produce cortisol.

Depression: When you're depressed, you may feel you can't feel anything because depression changes the way your brain processes emotions.

Medications: If you're taking medication for anxiety, depression, or another mental health condition, emotional numbness may be a side effect.

Grief: When you're grieving, it's normal to feel disconnected from your emotions because grief is a form of emotional pain. When you're in pain, it's natural to want to numb yourself.

Abuse: If you've been through abuse, it's not uncommon to feel you can't feel anything because abuse causes trauma. When you're traumatized, your brain may become numb to your emotions to protect you from further pain. Abuse can mean many things. It can be physical, sexual, emotional, or verbal abuse.

Drug use: When you abuse drugs, they change the way your brain processes emotions. This can lead to feeling emotionally numb. It can also lead to other mental health problems, such as anxiety and depression.

Emotional numbness can be a result of many factors. If you're struggling with emotional numbness, it's important to talk to a therapist who can help you identify the cause of your emotional numbness and develop a treatment plan.

How to Cope With Emotional Numbness

Struggling with emotional numbness can make you feel helpless, but you can engage in different techniques to feel better. In

DBT, many techniques can help you with your emotions. These skills are referred to as "emotion regulation skills." If you're feeling numb, it may be helpful to use some of these skills.

One of the most useful skills is called "opposite action." This means that when you're feeling a certain emotion, you do the opposite of what that emotion would tell you to do. For example, if you're feeling numb and disconnected from your emotions, the opposite action would tell you to do something that would make you feel more connected and emotionally engaged. This could mean reaching out to a friend or loved one, participating in an activity that you enjoy, or doing something that is meaningful to you.

Additionally, you could practice self-talk, which is another form of emotion regulation. This involves talking to yourself in a positive and supportive way. For example, you might tell yourself "It's okay to feel numb right now. I can get through this." This type of self-talk can help to reframe your experience in a more positive light and can help to increase your emotional resilience.

Lastly, it is important to practice self-care. This means taking care of yourself emotionally and physically. This can include factors like getting enough sleep, eating a balanced diet, and exercising regularly. When you take care of yourself, you're more likely to cope with difficult emotions.

To help with the challenges of emotion numbness, here are some tips:

- Identify your feelings.

- Talk to someone who will understand.

- Write down your thoughts and feelings.

- Express your emotions creatively.

- Seek professional help.

You might want to reach out for help if you're struggling and don't see any improvements. Many treatments are available and with the right treatment, you can start to feel better.

Listed below is an opposite action exercise to help you regulate your emotions.

Opposite Action Exercise

Instructions:

1. Read the following scenario and rate how distressing it is on a scale from 0 to 100.

2. Write down what you are feeling in response to the scenario.

3. Identify what the opposite action would be for each feeling you listed.

4. Practice the opposite action for each feeling.

Scenario: You are at a party, and you see someone you used to date. They are with someone else and seem happy.

Distress Rating	
Personal Response	
Opposite Action	

Practice Your Own Opposite Actions

Describe the scenario you will be working on in the space below and then follow the prompts below like you did for the exercise above.

Scenario

Distress Rating	
Personal Response	
Opposite Action	

Treating Emotional Numbness

You can combat emotional numbness in different ways. The best treatment option for you will depend on the cause of your emotional numbness.

Some common treatment options for emotional numbness include:

Psychotherapy: This is a type of therapy that can help you understand and work through your emotions.

Medication: If your emotional numbness is caused by depression or anxiety, medication may be helpful.

Self-care: Taking care of yourself is important when you're struggling with emotional numbness. Eat a healthy diet, exercise regularly, and get plenty of rest.

Support groups: Connecting with others who are going through similar experiences can be beneficial to your healing process. Online and in-person support groups are available to help you stay in your comfort zone but still receive assistance.

Additional Coping Tips

Here are a few additional tips to deal with emotional numbness:

Create and Maintain a Support System

Your support system is the people you rely on for help and

advice. When you're struggling with emotional numbness, it's important to have a strong support system. Your support system can include family, friends, and mental health professionals.

Talk About Your Feelings

When you talk about your emotions, it can help you understand them better. It can also help you feel less alone. You can talk about your feelings with your support system, a therapist, or in a support group.

Write Down Your Thoughts and Feelings

Writing down your experiences and how your thoughts and feelings were impacted can help you understand your emotions better, and it can be a way to express your emotions if you're struggling to talk about them.

Practice Self-Care

Self-care is important when dealing with emotional numbness. Take care of yourself physically and emotionally. This includes eating healthy, exercising, getting enough sleep, and taking breaks when you need them.

Seek Professional Help

If you're struggling to cope with emotional numbness, seek professional help. A mental health professional can diagnose and treat underlying conditions that may cause your emotional numbness. They can also provide you with tools and resources to help you cope.

Take Part in Physical Activities

Engaging in physical activity can be very helpful in reducing emotional numbness. Exercise can help reduce stress and improve your mood. It can also help you feel more connected to your body. Try to find an activity that you enjoy and make it part of your regular routine.

Find a Creative Outlet

Creative activities can help you relax when you struggle with emotional numbness. When you engage in creative activities, it can help you express your emotions, which can make you feel more connected to your body and the world around you. There are many creative outlets you can explore, such as painting, writing, photography, and music.

Get More Rest

Getting enough rest can help you fight against emotional numbness. Get plenty of sleep and take breaks during the day. You may also want to consider taking a vacation or staying home from work or school for a few days.

Lessen Stress in Your Life

Stress can make emotional numbness worse. If you're struggling with emotional numbness, try to identify and reduce the amount of stress in your life. This may include making changes to your lifestyle, such as exercise and relaxation. You may also want to consider seeking professional help to manage stress.

Create a Routine

Having a structured routine can be beneficial when you're dealing with emotional numbness because you can feel more in control of your life. It can also help you structure your day and make time for self-care.

Practice Mindful Techniques

Mindfulness can help you become more aware of your thoughts and feelings, which can help you combat emotional numbness. It can also help you accept your emotions and learn to cope healthily with them. Many mindfulness techniques are available for you to try, such as meditation, breathing exercises, and yoga.

DBT and CBT Techniques That Can Help

Many CBT and DBT techniques can be helpful when you're struggling with emotional numbness. These techniques can help you understand and manage your feelings. They can also help you develop healthy coping mechanisms. Some of the most common CBT and DBT techniques include:

Mindfulness: Mindfulness helps you tune into your emotions and feelings so you can accept them and cope with them properly.

Breathing exercises: Breathing exercises can help you relax and reduce stress. They can also help you control your emotions.

Visualization: You can use this skill to imagine yourself in a calm and peaceful place. It can also help you relax and reduce stress.

Progressive muscle relaxation: Progressive muscle relaxation can help you release tension from your body, which can also help you control your emotions.

Journaling: Journaling can help you express your thoughts and feelings. It can also help you understand your emotions and develop healthy coping mechanisms.

As you can see, many techniques are available that can help. Focus on doing what you enjoy so you can reap the most benefits and stay on track.

Key Takeaways

- Emotional numbness is a condition that can be caused by many factors, including trauma, stress, anxiety, and depression.

- Symptoms of emotion numbness include feeling

disconnected from your emotions, feeling unable to feel joy, and feeling isolated from others.

- You can cope with emotional numbness in a variety of ways. Some coping mechanisms include getting more rest, practicing mindful techniques, and journaling or other creative outlets. Other ways to cope with emotional numbness include seeking professional help, reducing stress, and creating a routine.

Chapter 7

Rogue Emotions

Rule number one: Don't sweat the small stuff. Rule number two: It's all small stuff.
—Robert S. Eliot

Have you ever felt so angry, frustrated or upset that you can't think straight? You may have felt like lashing out or just wanted to curl up in a ball and hide. Or maybe you've been in a funk for days, weeks or even months feeling sad, worried or anxious. These are all perfectly normal reactions to feeling overwhelmed emotionally. These are all what we call "rogue emotions." However, if you find your emotions are regularly running wild and affecting your day-to-day life, it might be time to focus on reframing those emotions. In this chapter, you will learn:

- About rogue emotions.

- The causes and symptoms of rogue emotions.

- Emotional sensitivity and distress.

- How to overcome rogue emotions.

What Are Rogue Emotions?

Rogue emotions are intense, negative emotions that feel out of control. They can come on suddenly and take over your thoughts, body, and behavior. Rogue emotions can be short-lived or last for a long time. They can make you feel you're in a fog or on autopilot. When you're in the throes of a rogue emotion, you may feel you're not in control of your own life.

You may make impulsive decisions, say things you don't mean, or act in ways that are out of character for you. Rogue emotions can cause you to lose focus, make mistakes, and feel disconnected from those around us. They can also lead to problems in relationships and at work.

Some common rogue emotions are:

- Anger
- Anxiety
- Depression
- Fear
- Frustration
- Grief
- Guilt

- Jealousy
- Loneliness
- Rejection

What Are the Symptoms of Rogue Emotions?

The symptoms of rogue emotions can vary depending on the emotion you're experiencing. For instance, if you're feeling angry, you may have a tight chest, clenched fists, and feel you're ready to explode. If you're feeling anxious, you may have a racing heart, feel short of breath, and feel you're going to faint.

Some common symptoms include:

- Feeling out of control
- Feeling like you're going crazy
- Feeling like you're going to die
- Feeling disconnected from yourself
- Feeling numb
- Feeling like everything is a blur

What Are the Causes of Rogue Emotions?

There are potential causes of rogue emotions. Some people may be more prone to them because of their genes or biology. Others may have experienced trauma or stressful life events that have triggered the emotions. For example, someone who witnessed a violent act may have intense feelings of fear and anxiety. Or someone who lost a loved one may feel overwhelming sadness and grief. Some people may have a chemical imbalance in their brain that contributes to their emotions. Additionally, social factors like upbringing, environment, and culture can also play a role.

What Are the Treatments for Rogue Emotions?

If you're struggling to manage your rogue emotions, a variety of treatment options are available. CBT can teach you how to identify and change the thoughts and behaviors that contribute to your emotions. DBT teaches skills like mindfulness and emotional regulation that can help you control your emotions. Medication can also be used to treat the symptoms of rogue emotions. Antidepressants, anti-anxiety medication, and mood stabilizers are all commonly prescribed.

In DBT, a handful of acronyms are used to describe emotions. Two popular ones are ABC PLEASE and STOP. According the Therapistaid, ABC PLEASE stands for:

- **A**ccumulating positive emotions
- **B**uild Mastery
- **C**ope Ahead
- Treat **p**hysical i**ll**nesses
- Balanced **e**ating
- **A**void mood altering drugs
- Follow a healthy **s**leep schedule
- **E**xercise regularly (Linehan, n.d.)

Accumulating positive emotions: With this skill, you work on identifying and experiencing more positive emotions in your life. This can help offset the negative emotions and give you a more balanced emotional state. The goal is to participate in activities that make you feel good regularly.

Build mastery: This skill is all about taking control of your life and building confidence in yourself. The goal is to set small, achievable goals and then accomplish them. This can help you feel more capable and in control, which can offset negative emotions.

Cope ahead: This skill is about planning for difficult situations so that you're better prepared to deal with them. The goal is to expect potential triggers for your emotions and have a plan in place to deal with them. This can help you feel more prepared and less likely to be overwhelmed by your emotions.

Treat physical illnesses: Your physical health is as equally important as your mental health. The better you feel physically, the better you'll be able to cope with negative emotions.

Balanced eating: Eating a balanced diet is essential for maintaining your physical and mental health. Eating healthy foods can help you feel better physically and give you the energy you need to deal with negative emotions.

Avoid mood-altering drugs: Mood-altering drugs can include alcohol, drugs, and tobacco. These substances can make your emotions worse and should be avoided.

Follow a healthy sleep schedule: Getting enough sleep is important for your physical and mental health. When you're well-rested, you'll be better able to cope with negative emotions.

Exercise regularly: Exercise releases endorphins, which have mood-boosting effects. When you exercise regularly, you'll feel better physically and mentally, which can help offset negative emotions.

Listed below in an ABC PLEASE exercise to help you incorporate these skills today!

ABC PLEASE Exercise

Try this exercise to help you practice the ABC PLEASE skill.

1. Make a list of five positive emotions that you want to cultivate in your life. Examples might include happiness, joy, love, peace, or contentment.

2. For each emotion, brainstorm three activities that you can do to experience that emotion more often.

3. Make a plan to do one activity from each emotion every day for the next week.

4. After you've completed the week, reflect on how you felt. Did you notice a difference in your emotional state? Did you find it easier to cope with negative emotions?

Emotions	Activities

STOP Skill

The other popular acronym, STOP, stands for

- Stop
- Take a step back

- Observe

- Proceed mindfully (linehan, n.d.-b)

Stop: When you're feeling overwhelmed by your emotions, it can be helpful to simply stop. Literally stop moving, and don't say or do anything. By taking a moment to stop, you can avoid resorting to your knee-jerk reaction. This can help you avoid making the situation worse or making a decision that you'll later regret.

Take a step back: Once you've stopped, it's important to take a step back from the situation. This means observing your emotions or the situation without judgment. Simply notice how you're feeling without trying to change it. However, don't allow your emotions to influence how you act. This can help you get some perspective on the situation and avoid getting caught up in your feelings.

Observe: Once you've taken a step back, observe the situation or your emotions without judgment. What do you see? What do you hear? What do you feel? Simply notice what's happening without trying to change it. Don't jump to conclusions, and look at the facts. This can help you gain some insight into your emotions and the situation.

Proceed mindfully: After you've taken a step back and observed the situation, you can proceed mindfully. This means making a deliberate decision about how you want to respond. Consider your options and choose the best course of action.

Stay cool, calm, and collected to avoid reacting impulsively to your emotions.

STOP Skill Exercise One

Try this exercise to help you practice the STOP skill.

1. Make a list of five difficult emotions that you often experience. Examples might include anger, sadness, anxiety, or jealousy.

2. For each emotion, brainstorm three situations that tend to trigger that emotion.

3. Make a plan to use the STOP skill the next time you're in each of those situations.

4. After you've used the skill, reflect on how it went. Did it help you cope with your emotions? Did it prevent you from making a decision that you later regretted?

Emotions list	

Emotion 1:

Situation 1:	
Situation 2:	
Situation 3:	

Emotion 2:

Situation 1:	
Situation 2:	

Situation 3:	

Emotion 3:

Situation 1:	
Situation 2:	
Situation 3:	

Emotion 4:

Situation 1:	

Situation 2:	
Situation 3:	

Emotion 5:

Situation 1:	
Situation 2:	
Situation 3:	

STOP Skill Exercise Two

Think of a recent situation where you felt overwhelmed by your emotions. How did you handle it? Then, consider how you could've used STOP to deal with the situation more effectively.

1. What was the situation?

2. What emotions were you feeling?

3. What was your knee-jerk reaction?

4. Which STOP skills could you have used instead?

5. How do you think the situation would've gone if you had used STOP?

What Is Emotional Sensitivity?

Emotional sensitivity is the ability to feel emotions deeply. It's a trait that can be both positive and negative. On the plus side, emotional sensitivity allows you to feel things deeply and connect with others. You're in tune with your own emotions, and you can pick up on the emotions of those around you.

On the downside, emotional sensitivity can make you more prone to anxiety, depression, and other mental health issues. You're more likely to be hurt by someone's words or actions, and you might have a hard time coping with stress and negative emotions. If you're emotionally sensitive, it's important to find healthy ways to deal with your emotions. Emotional sensitivity is not a bad thing. It just means that you need to be extra careful about taking care of yourself.

What Are the Symptoms of Emotional Sensitivity?

While the symptoms of emotional sensitivity can vary from person to person, some symptoms are more common than others. For example, some people may feel overwhelmed by their emotions, while others may feel like they're on an emotional roller coaster. Additionally, some people may have difficulty regulating their emotions, and are easily triggered by things that remind them of their trauma.

What Are the Treatments for Emotional Sensitivity?

You can overcome emotional sensitivity using a variety of methods. Some common treatments include therapy, medication, and lifestyle changes. Therapy can help you manage your emotions and medication can help to balance your chemicals and hormones that may contribute to your feelings. Lifestyle changes can help to reduce stress and improve your overall health. You can even use the worksheets throughout this guide to help you DBT and CBT skills. Everyone is different, so it is important to find what works best for you.

Being Sensitive to Emotional Stimuli

Emotional sensitivity is a trait that refers to how easily someone is emotionally aroused. This can mean that you cry easily, get angry easily, or simply feel things more deeply than others. As for emotional stimuli, this can refer to anything that has the potential to provoke an emotional response. This can include things like:

- A moving or sad story
- An intense movie scene
- A loved one in pain
- A difficult life event

Of course, not all emotional stimuli will have the same effect on all people. What affects one person deeply may not faze another person at all. However, if you're emotionally sensitive, you're more likely than most to be impacted by emotional stimuli. This means that you may need to take extra care of yourself during stressful times, and be mindful of the media you consume, but it also means that you're likely to be more compassionate and attuned to the emotions of others. So even though being emotionally sensitive can sometimes be challenging, it's also a gift.

It's important to remember that you can't control how you feel. If you're feeling overwhelmed, give yourself permission to take a break from the emotional stimulus. This might mean turning off the news, avoiding social media, or taking a few days off from work.

You might also find it helpful to talk to someone about what you're going through. Talking to a therapist or counselor can help you process your emotions and develop coping strategies.

Adapting to Emotional Stimuli

If you're emotionally sensitive, it's tough to deal with all the conflicting emotions that come your way daily. You might feel like you're on an emotional roller coaster, and it's hard to know how to react when you're feeling overwhelmed. However, you can help yourself cope with emotional stimuli using different techniques. First, it's important to identify your triggers. What are the things that tend to set off your emotions?

After becoming aware of your triggers, you can start to work on avoiding them or at least preparing yourself for them in advance. It's also important to learn how to deal with your emotions healthily. This might mean talking to a friend or therapist about how you're feeling or finding a creative outlet that helps you express yourself.

Lastly, don't be afraid to ask for help when you need it. There's no shame in admitting that you need some extra support to deal with your emotions. By learning how to adapt to emotional stimuli, you can start to take control of your life and feel more confident and happier.

Additionally, if you're emotionally sensitive, it's important to learn how to adapt to emotional stimuli. This might mean:

- Learning how to take breaks from emotional stimuli such as the news or social media.

- Developing a self-care routine that includes things like exercise, relaxation, and healthy eating.

- Learning how to set boundaries with others, like saying no to invitations or requests that you're not comfortable with.

- Learning how to talk about your emotions healthily by practicing assertive communication.

- Learning how to manage your stress levels by using relaxation techniques such as yoga, meditation, or by incorporating other DBT or CBT skills like breathing exercises.

What Is Emotional Distress?

You might feel emotional distress when you're going through a tough time in your life. Maybe you're dealing with the death of a loved one, or you're experiencing financial difficulties.

Whatever the case may be, it's normal to feel overwhelmed by your emotions during times of stress. However, emotional distress can interfere with your ability to function in daily life.

If you're struggling with emotional distress, you might find it hard to:

- Concentrate at work or school
- Take care of your responsibilities at home
- Interact with friends and family
- Enjoy your hobbies and interests

Warning and Risk Factors of Emotional Distress

Everyone experiences emotional distress at some point in their lives. This is a common reaction to life stressors. However, when emotional distress becomes chronic, it can lead to serious mental health problems.

Warning signs of emotional distress include:

- Feeling overwhelmed by emotions
- Feeling unable to function in daily life
- Withdrawing from friends and family

- Losing interest in hobbies and interests

- Experiencing changes in appetite or sleep

- Feeling hopeless or helpless

- Feeling like you can't cope

Emotional distress can be a normal response, but when it becomes excessive, it can become debilitating. A popular way to combat these feelings is to practice radical acceptance. This means accepting things as they are, rather than how you want them to be. It can be a hard concept to grasp, but it is worth it to try. Below is a worksheet to help you practice radical acceptance.

Radical Acceptance Worksheet

When you encounter a challenging situation, it's easy to allow your thoughts to ruminate over how "unfair" life is or believe that you shouldn't have to experience this turmoil. However, most times, life is out of your control, and that type of thinking can make you feel worse. Practicing radical acceptance can help you develop a healthier way of thinking. Rather than focusing on how things "should be," you learn to observe the situation and accept it for what it is: a challenge beyond your control that you have to overcome.

Practicing radical acceptance doesn't mean you have to like or even agree with the situation, it just means that you will work through it, which can lead to feeling less anxious and more in control. Below is an example and prompts to help you get started with practicing radical acceptance.

Example:

Scenario
You've just been diagnosed with a chronic illness.

Default thoughts	Radical acceptance thoughts
Why me? I can't believe this is happening! I don't deserve this!	This is my current reality and I have to accept it. I will do whatever it takes to manage my illness. I am still the same person, even though I have this

	diagnosis.

Create your own:

Scenario

Default thoughts	Radical acceptance thoughts

Scenario

Default thoughts	Radical acceptance thoughts

Can You Experience Both Rogue Emotions and Emotional Numbness?

In theory, yes. However, in general most people lean towards one experience more than the other. Some people may experience rogue emotions in certain situations and emotional numbness in others. For example, a person may experience rogue emotions when they are triggered by a memory of a past trauma, but in day-to-day life, they may become numb and disconnected from their emotions.

Key Takeaways

- Rogue emotions are intense, out-of-control emotions that
- can be triggered by things like memories or stressful situations.
- Emotional distress is a common reaction to life stressors. However, when it becomes chronic and takes over your life, it can lead to serious mental health problems.
- When you feel emotions deeply, even if those feelings aren't yours, that is emotional sensitivity.
- To combat these emotions, you can adopt practices to adapt to emotional stimuli. This might mean:
  - Taking breaks from media that contributes to emotional sensitivity.
  - Creating a self-care routine that includes activities you enjoy and that would benefit your health.
  - Setting boundaries with friends, family or other people in your life.
  - Talking about your emotions appropriately by practicing assertive communication.
  - Learning how to oversee your stress levels by using relaxation techniques.

- STOP and ABC PLEASE are acronyms that can help you remember what to do when you're feeling overwhelmed by emotions.

Chapter 8

The Danger Zone

Stress is an ignorant state. It believes that everything is an emergency. Nothing is that important.
—Natalie Goldberg

The point of no return for people suffering from severe forms of anxiety, depression, and bipolar disorders seems to be when they cannot control their actions anymore. This can happen because the brain gets stuck in a terrible state or pattern that is difficult to break out of on its own without help. Often, this is referred to as the "danger zone" because it is when people are at their most vulnerable and need help the most. Getting out of the danger zone requires asking for assistance and cooperating with a treatment plan. In this chapter, you will learn:

- What the danger zone is.

- Why the danger zone exists.

- How to combat the challenges that come with being in the danger zone.

What Is the Danger Zone?

The danger zone is a term used to describe the space between an event that causes anxiety and the reaction to that event. This is the space where anxiety and panic attacks live. In the danger zone, the brain is in a heightened state of alertness and the body is in a state of fight-or-flight. The zone is the space where the brain and the body are preparing for danger.

The danger zone is a space where the brain is trying to protect the body from harm. But sometimes, the danger zone can be more harmful than the event that caused the anxiety in the first place because the brain is not always good at distinguishing between real and imagined threats. So, the danger zone can become a space where the brain is constantly on the lookout for danger, even when there is no real threat, which in turn can cause you to become more anxious and depressed as you "fail" to overcome that danger.

How Do You Get Into the Danger Zone?

The danger zone is not a place you enter willingly. You are drawn into the danger zone by your anxiety or fears. Anxiety is like a magnet that pulls you into the danger zone and keeps you there if you're not strong enough to repel against it. The more you try to fight anxiety, the more it pulls you into the danger zone.

Why Does the Danger Zone Exist?

The great thing about DBT is that it provides a way for you to understand that although your emotions or thoughts don't have a clear connection, there's still a reason for the behavior. The danger zone exists because of the way your brain is wired. Your brain is programmed to protect you from harm, and because of the experiences you've had in your life, you might find harm in different areas.

Some people are more prone to anxiety than others because of the way their brains are wired, and some people are more prone to anxiety because of their experiences. For example, if you grew up in a family where there was a lot of yelling and fighting, you might be more prone to anxiety because your brain learned that yelling and fighting are dangerous. Those actions are negative repercussions to a particular stimulus.

If you grew up in a family where there was a lot of love and support, you might be less prone to anxiety because your brain learned that love and support are safe. When you're uncomfortable and unable to cope with your emotions, you might enter the danger zone in order to numb and protect yourself from the pain.

Common Reasons for Entering the Danger Zone

The danger zone is a place that protects you from harm. At times, specific situations or people can cause you to enter this zone. For instance, social media or the news might be full of stories about violence, which can cause you to enter the danger zone.

Or, you might have a fight with a friend or family member, which can also cause you to enter the danger zone. If you're in an abusive relationship, you might find that you're constantly in the danger zone because you're constantly exposed to an environment that is full of violence and danger.

Common reasons for entering the danger zone can be divided into two categories:

- External factors, like the news or social media

- Internal factors, like a fight with a friend or family member

Other reasons for entering the danger zone can include:

- A traumatic event, like a car accident

- An anxiety disorder

- Depression

- Bipolar disorder

- Ptsd

- Avoidance

- Numbing

- Dissociation
- Escape
- Self-harm
- Substance abuse

What Are the Symptoms of the Danger Zone?

The symptoms of the danger zone vary from person to person, but there are some common symptoms that people experience when they are stuck in this zone. These symptoms include:

- Feeling out of control
- Feeling like you are going to die
- Feeling like you are going to lose control
- Feeling like you are going to faint
- Feeling like you are going to vomit
- Feeling like the world is spinning
- Feeling like you are not in your body
- Feeling disconnected from reality
- Feeling emotional numbness or rogue emotions

When you're in the danger zone, you might experience similar or different symptoms. However, if you're concerned, you may want to consider reaching out for help or incorporating more CBT and DBT practices into your life.

How to Manage Those Symptoms?

The best way to stay out of the danger zone is to prevent yourself from entering it in the first place. This means being aware of the things that might trigger your anxiety or stress. It also means having a plan for what you will do if you start to feel anxious or stressed.

If you know that watching the news makes you anxious, then don't watch the news. Try to avoid certain people if you know they make you anxious. If you can't avoid them, then set boundaries with them.

Having a plan might mean making a list of things that help you calm down. It might also mean having the number of a mental health professional that you can call if you start to feel like you're in the danger zone.

Some things that might help you calm down are:

- Taking a bath
- Reading a book
- Going for a walk
- Listening to music

- Doing yoga

- Writing in a journal

To manage the symptoms of the danger zone, you can:

- Identify the triggers that cause you to enter the danger zone. These triggers can be different for different people. Some common triggers include stress, anxiety, fear, and flashbacks.

- Avoid the triggers. Avoidance can be difficult to do, but it is important to avoid the things that trigger your anxiety.

- Learn the warning signs of the danger zone. These warning signs can help you know when you are about to enter the danger zone. Some common warning signs include feeling out of control, feeling like you are going to die, feeling like you are going to lose control, and feeling like you are going to faint.

- Seek help from a mental health professional if you are experiencing the symptoms of the danger zone or feel stuck. A mental health professional can help you learn how to cope with the symptoms of the danger zone.

What Are the Consequences of the Danger Zone?

When you're feeling negatively, the consequences of the danger zone can be very harmful. This is because the danger zone can lead to

- Panic attacks

- Anxiety disorders

- Depression

- Eating disorders

You might withdraw from activities that you used to enjoy or avoid social situations altogether. The danger zone can also lead to a decline in work performance and difficulty maintaining relationships. Keep an eye on your symptoms and ensure they don't get worse.

The consequences of the danger zone can be serious. If the danger zone is not managed effectively, it can lead to:

- Self-harm

- Harm to others

- Suicidal thoughts or behaviors

- Hospitalization

- Death

- Substance abuse

If you are in the danger zone and experiencing any of these

concerns, you may want to speak with a mental health professional. They will be able to help you manage the symptoms and prevent the serious consequences of being in the danger zone.

What Can You Do if You Are in the Danger Zone?

Being in this zone can feel like the end of the world, but luckily you can dig your way out of the danger zone. Often when you're stuck in this zone, you suffer negative consequences as a result. However, to get out of it, most of the time you need to do the opposite of what your natural inclination is telling you to do.

If you find yourself stuck in the danger zone, you might find it helpful to seek help from a mental health professional. They will help you manage the symptoms you may experience and prevent serious consequences or your return to the danger zone in the future.

If you are in the danger zone, you can help yourself by:

- Breathing deeply
- Focusing on something in the room
- Repeating a mantra or affirmation
- Visualization

- Moving your body

Practice Self-Soothing Techniques

Self-soothing is a term that is used to describe the act of calming yourself down. When you soothe yourself, you are essentially giving yourself a break from the stressor that is causing you to feel overwhelmed. This can be done in a number of ways, but some common self-soothing techniques include incorporating your five senses.

Listed below is an example of how you can use your five senses to practice self-soothing techniques. After you review the example, create a list of activities you enjoy that incorporate your five senses to practice when you feel overwhelmed.

Example:

Sight	Look at pictures or videos that make you happy.
Sound	Listen to calming music or sounds.
Smell	Smell soothing aromatherapy or essential oils.
Taste	Eat your favorite foods or drink a warm beverage.

Touch	Give yourself a hug, use a soft blanket or stuffed animal, or get a massage.

Create your own: Make a list of activities that you can engage in when you are in the danger zone.

Sight	
Sound	

Smell	
Taste	
Touch	

How Can You Prevent the Danger Zone?

The truth is, as the name suggests, the danger zone is quite dangerous. As mentioned before, entering this zone can be more detrimental to your health than what sets it off. Often, getting out of this zone can seem impossible. Hence, the best thing you can do is to prevent yourself from entering the danger zone in the first place.

Prevention is key with the danger zone. To prevent entering the danger zone, you can practice

- Managing stress
- Relaxation techniques
- Getting regular exercise
- Eating a healthy diet
- Getting enough sleep
- Dbt and cbt skills

Why Is Prevention Important?

The danger zone can be very harmful and the more you enter this space or the longer you stay in this space, the more damage it does. That's why prevention is so important. Prevention allows you to avoid the danger zone altogether or at least minimize the time you spend in this space. When you prevent the danger zone, you protect yourself from the harmful consequences that can come from this space. When you prevent entering this zone, then you can avoid:

- Panic attacks

- Anxiety disorders

- Depression

- Eating disorders

- Self-harm

- Harm to others

- Hospitalization

- Death

Additionally, prevention can help you maintain your quality of life. When you prevent the danger zone, you can:

- Continue working

- Maintain relationships

- Participate in activities you enjoy

Prevention is key when it comes to the danger zone. By taking steps to prevent the danger zone, you can avoid the harmful consequences of this state. When you learn to prevent entering this zone, you can enjoy your life without the worry of the harmful consequences that come from this space.

How Can DBT and CBT Skills Help Me With the Danger Zone?

DBT and CBT skills aim to help you manage the symptoms of the danger zone. In fact, being in this state of "rock bottom" is when DBT skills have proven to be most helpful because it is the point of no return. When you're in the danger zone, you might feel like you're out of control. The goal of DBT and CBT skills is to help you feel more in control of your thoughts and emotions. They can also help prevent the serious consequences of the danger zone. Some skills that can be helpful in the danger zone include:

- Mindfulness

- Distress tolerance

- Emotion regulation

What Do I Need to Do to Get Out of or Prevent Entering the Danger Zone?

Confront your fears: Once you have identified your fears, it is time to confront them. This may sound traumatic, and facing your fears requires courage, but it is necessary to overcome the emotions that fears bring.

You can start by facing your fears in small steps. For example, if you are afraid of heights, you can start by looking at pictures or videos of high places. Once you are comfortable with that, you can move on to standing on a stool or going to the top of a small hill. It is important to remember that you may not overcome your fear completely, but by facing your fears, you can learn to control your reactions to them.

Change your thinking: One of the fundamental ways to prevent the danger zone is to change the way you think about your anxiety. For example, if you are afraid of social gatherings, you might tell yourself that parties are safe and that you have nothing to worry about.

You can also try to reframe your thoughts in a more positive light. For example, instead of thinking *I'm going to have a panic attack on the plane*, you can tell yourself *I can handle this*.

Practice relaxation techniques: Relaxation techniques are helpful in reducing the symptoms of anxiety and stress. Some of the most popular relaxation techniques include:

- Deep breathing
- Progressive muscle relaxation

- Visualization

These techniques can help you slow down your heart rate and breathing, and to feel more in control of your anxiety.

Get regular exercise: Exercise can be helpful in reducing stress and anxiety. It can also help to improve your mood and overall sense of well-being.

Eat a healthy diet: Eating a proper diet is important for overall health and well-being. It can also help reduce stress and anxiety.

Get enough sleep: Getting enough sleep is important for overall health and well-being, which can also reduce stress and anxiety.

If you are struggling to get out of the danger zone, or if you are having thoughts of harming yourself or others, don't be afraid to ask for help. A mental health professional can help you understand and manage your symptoms and can provide you with the tools you need to recover.

Key Takeaways

- The danger zone is a state of extreme anxiety or stress that can lead to harmful consequences.
- Some CBT and DBT skills that can help you avoid or escape the danger zone include mindfulness, distress

tolerance, and emotion regulation.

- Self-soothing is a technique that can prompt you to calm down in the moment and prevent the escalation of anxiety or stress, which can be helpful when you're in the danger zone. Using the five senses to self-sooth is an easy and effective way to practice cultivating positive emotions.

- Avoiding the danger zone is the best way to prevent the harmful consequences that can occur when you're in this state. The danger zone can be prevented by changing the way you think about your anxiety and practicing relaxation techniques, but if the emotions arise, you now have all the tools you need when they do.

Chapter 9

There's Nothing to Worry About

There is only one way to happiness and that is to cease worrying about things which are beyond the power of our will.
—Epictetus

To be frank, worrying is normal. Remember the caveman brain? Worrying has been ingrained in your brain from the beginning of time. It's an emotion that everyone experiences from time to time. What isn't normal, however, is letting worries take control of our lives. In this chapter you will learn the following:

- Why worrying can be more detrimental than helpful.

- How to reduce your worries.

- Common thought distortions that add to worrying.

For some people, anxiety and worrying can be so constant and overwhelming that they affect their daily lives. It is important to remember, however, that you don't live in the stone ages anymore. Think about it: with the last thing you worried about, did the world end? Did your life fall apart or change in a major way? Most likely, the answer is no.

So what's the point of worrying then? If it does nothing to change the situation, why does everybody keep doing it? Worrying made sense thousands of years ago, when your life depended on it and it was the only way to support yourself or your family, but now, in the modern world, it's nothing more than a waste of time and energy.

The answer is actually quite simple: you worry because you think it will make the situation better. Subconsciously, you think that if you worry enough, you'll be able to change the outcome or prevent something bad from happening.

However, worrying does the exact opposite. It doesn't make the situation better; it makes it worse. Worrying creates more stress, which then leads to more anxiety and more worrying. It's a never-ending cycle that only makes the situation worse.

Sure, it's possible that worry can lead to a brainstorming session that solves the problem, but more often than not, worry just leads to more anxiety and stress. So how do you break the cycle?

Actually, it's not about breaking the cycle; rather, it's about stopping the cycle before it even starts, just like the danger zone. Think about it—what are you worried about? Did you make a mistake? Are you going to fail? Is someone going to find out a secret?

These worries are based on the future, and the future is something that you can't control. No matter how much you worry, you can't change what's going to happen. The only thing you can control is yourself. Instead of worrying about what's going to happen or what happened, be proactive and focus on what you can do right now, at this very moment.

The first step is to recognize your worries. It's important to catch yourself in the act so that you can stop it. Once you realize you're worrying, the next step is to ask yourself why you're doing it. What are you trying to accomplish by worrying?

Here are three questions you can ask yourself:

1. What's the worst that could happen?

2. What are the chances of that happening?

3. Can I do anything to prevent it from happening?

If you can answer all three questions, then you'll know that there's no reason to worry. Worrying is only helpful if it leads to a solution. If not, then it's just a waste of time and energy. Of course, that's easier said than done. Worrying is a hard habit to break, but the more you practice, the easier it will become.

The next step is to let it go. Letting go can be tough—you want to solve the problem and letting it go won't give you the solution you crave, but you can't control the future. The only thing you can control is yourself and how you react to the situation.

One way to let go of your worry is to practice mindfulness by meditating or doing some deep breathing exercises. This will help you clear your mind and relax your body. Once you're feeling more relaxed, you can think more clearly.

Another way to let go of worry is to come up with a plan. If you're worried about failing, come up with a plan to study more or get help from a tutor. If you're worried about someone finding out, come up with a plan to keep it a secret. Having a plan will help to ease your worry because you'll know that you're taking action to prevent the worst from happening.

Here are a few additional tips to help you stop worrying:

1. **Set aside a specific time to worry.**

Ok, yes, worrying can be a waste of time. At the same time, your brain needs to work through the turmoil. It might seem silly, but compare this to a diet. For the most part in a diet, you're supposed to eat healthily 80-90% of the time, and then 10-20% of the time you're allowed to indulge. Some people have a cheat day once a week, month, or whenever works best for them. It's ok to give into some bad habits occasionally, especially if you're doing it for the overall good.

Worrying is the same way. You don't want to do it all the time, but setting aside a specific time will help to ease your worry. Maybe you put aside ten minutes every day to list all the worries that came about. Maybe you do it once a week. Getting your thoughts and emotions out can be healthy, but when done in moderation.

2. Talk to someone who will understand.

Some people like to talk about their problems, while others prefer to keep them to themselves. If you're the type of person who likes to talk about your worries, find someone who will understand and can offer helpful advice. This could be a friend, family member, therapist, or anyone else who you feel comfortable talking to.

Sometimes it's helpful to see things from a different perspective. However, keep in mind the first step. Putting a time cap on your talk time frame is wise. Don't allow it to consume you. Take advantage of the support to bounce problem-solving ideas. However, if there's a consensus that the situation likely cannot be changed, then it might be best to accept it and move on.

3. Write it down.

If you're someone who prefers not to talk about your worries, then writing them down might be a better option for you. You can journal, blog, or even just write a list. Writing down your worries can help you organize your thoughts and figure out what's really bothering you. It can also be a way to release your emotions without burdening anyone else, and like the previous step, setting a time limit is key. You don't want writing to become another worry.

4. Distract yourself.

Sometimes, the best way to stop worrying is to simply distract yourself. Remember to be mindful. Your thoughts and emotions are temporary states. They come and go—if you allow them, that is. What this means is that a thought can float into your brain at any moment, but it can also leave just as quickly if you don't hold on to it.

So if a worry pops into your head, try to think about something else. Maybe you focus on a project you're working on or something that's coming up that you're excited about. Or maybe you focus on the present moment and what's around you. Paying attention to your senses can help to ground you in the here and now. Practice the exercises in this workbook to help you distract yourself and practice healthy coping techniques.

Thought Distortions

To challenge the thoughts that contribute to worries and anxiety, you have many options. This includes identifying and challenging thought distortions. Thought distortions are ways that our thinking can become biased, which can lead to inaccurate conclusions.

If you're able to identify the thought distortions in your thinking, you can then challenge them and see things in a more realistic light. Many reasons we worry and become anxious are because we've blown things out of proportion or we're only considering the negative outcome. By challenging these thought distortions, we can see things more clearly.

Here are some common thought distortions:

- All-or-nothing thinking

    - Situations, people, or experiences are viewed only in black and white, with no shades of gray. For example, you might think that if you don't get the promotion, you're a complete failure.

- Overgeneralization

    - You see a single event as part of a never-ending pattern. For example, you might think that because you failed the test, you're doomed to fail everything. These thoughts often include words like "always" and "never."

- Mental filter

    - You concentrate only on the negative aspects of a situation while bypassing all the positive aspects. For example, you might only remember the times you've been rejected, instead of all the times you've been accepted.

- Disqualifying the positive

    - You dismiss the positive experiences in your life by telling yourself that they don't count. For example, you might write off a compliment by saying that the other person was just being nice.

- Jumping to conclusions

  - You conclude without having all the facts. For example, you might think that someone is mad at you because they didn't return your text right away, even though there could be a perfectly innocent explanation.

- Mind reading

  - You assume you know what other people are thinking, with no evidence to back it up. For example, you might think that your boss is going to fire you because she was looking at you funny.

- Fortune telling

  - You predict things will turn out badly, with no evidence to support your claim. For example, you might think that you're going to fail the test, even though you haven't studied yet.

- Catastrophizing

  - You think about the worst potential outcome of a situation, no matter how unlikely it is. For example, you might think that if you don't get the job, you'll never be able to find a job.

- Emotional reasoning

  - You think that because you feel a certain way, it must be

true. For example, you might think that because you're feeling anxious, there must be something wrong.

- "Should" statements
  - You unnecessarily pressure yourself by having unrealistic expectations. For example, you might tell yourself that you "should" be able to handle this stressor with no problem.
- Labeling
  - You label yourself based on your mistakes and shortcomings. For example, you might call yourself a "loser" because you failed the test.
- Personalization
  - You hold yourself responsible for things that are out of your control. For example, you might think that it's your fault that your friend is having a bad day.

By identifying these thought distortions in your thinking, you can challenge them. For example, if you're catastrophizing about a situation, you can remind yourself that you're only considering the worst probable outcome, which is unlikely to happen. If you're labeling yourself, you can remind yourself that everyone makes mistakes and that you're not defined by your mistakes.

Once you challenge these thought distortions, you'll start to see things more clearly. You'll be able to better manage your anxiety and worry less about things that are out of your control.

Overcoming Thought Distortions

If you're struggling with anxiety, learning how to manage your thoughts can help you overcome the challenges you experience. That's where cognitive behavioral therapy and dialectical behavioral therapy skills come in. These therapies have techniques designed to help you identify and challenge your thought distortions.

With CBT, you can identify your negative thoughts and develop more realistic perspectives. Essentially you would learn how to challenge your thought distortions by asking yourself questions such as "Is there evidence to support this thought?" or "What is the worst thing that could happen and how likely is it to happen?"

With DBT, you would learn skills to help you cope with negative emotions such as being mindful or practicing acceptance. You would also learn how to regulate your emotions by identifying your triggers and using self-soothing techniques such as deep breathing or visualization.

By learning how to identify and challenge your thought distortions, you can start to see things more clearly, and by learning how to cope with negative emotions and regulate your emotions, you can start to feel better.

Thought Distortion Worksheet

Below is a worksheet with scenarios. Read the scenario and thought distortion that accompanies it. Then determine how you can spin the thought in a more positive or realistic direction. The first one is done for you as an example.

Scenario	Thought Distortion	Realistic Thoughts
You're at a party, and you see someone you know. You say hi, but they don't respond.	They must hate me.	They might not have heard me. Or they might be preoccupied with something else.
You're in a meeting, and you make a mistake.	I'm so stupid.	
You're on a date and the person you're with seems to be lost in	They must not be interested in me.	

thought.		
You're at a restaurant, and the server gets your order wrong.	This is such a disaster. My needs are invisible to others.	

Now, using your own thoughts and situations, describe your experience, the thought distortion you had and reframe it to be more neutral or positive, like you did in the exercises above.

Scenario	Thought Distortion	Realistic Thoughts

Key Takeaways

- Worrying was originally useful in the caveman days where your survival depended on it. Nowadays, worrying is often irrational and can cause more harm than good.

- Cognitive distortions are patterns of thinking that lead to inaccurate perceptions of reality, which can lead to stress and more worrying.

- Worrying can come from a myriad of challenges,

including different thought distortions, such as all-or-nothing thinking and overgeneralization. By identifying the thought distortions in your thinking, you can start to challenge them.

Chapter 10

Experience Is Your Guru

Anxiety's like a rocking chair. It gives you something to do, but it doesn't get you very far.
—Jodi Picoult

When you're learning something new, it's difficult to implement different techniques and track your progress. Learning new skills can be an overwhelming process. Are you doing it right? Are you reaping the benefits? This is especially true when you're first starting out, and everything seems equally essential. How can you tell if you're making progress? In this chapter, you will learn:

- The importance of experience.

- How to gain experience.

- Tips for success.

The only way to get better at something is to practice it, and the only way to gauge your progress is to measure it. Therefore, keeping a CBT workbook, for example, can be an invaluable asset during your journey of personal growth. It's important to have a foundation of understanding to build upon. Otherwise, you'll just be learning surface-level information and not really internalizing anything.

That's why experience is such an important teacher. Once you've gone through something yourself, you have a much better understanding of it than if you had just read or heard about it, and that's why this CBT workbook helps you track your progress and ensure that you're actually internalizing the concepts you're learning. So how do you get experience?

There are two ways: by doing, and by reflecting. Both are essential for learning. If you only do, you'll miss out on the insights gained from reflection, and if you only reflect, you'll never put your learning into practice. The key is to find a balance between the two.

Experience by Doing

The best way to learn something is by doing it. This gives you first-hand experience with the material and helps you understand it on a deeper level. It also allows you to immediately apply what you've learned in a real-world setting.

To gain experience by doing, you can:

Get engaged: The best way to learn something is to actually do it. If you want to learn how to bake, for example, the best way to do that is to get in the kitchen and start baking!

Try out different techniques and see which one's work best for you. The exercises in this book provide you with hands-on experience with the concepts you're learning. Implement them in your own life and see how they work for you. The more you try new techniques, the more you can hone your newfound skills.

Use a simulator or practice visualization techniques: If you can't actually do the thing you're trying to learn (if you want to learn how to fly a plane but don't have access to one, for example), you can use a simulator or practice visualization techniques. This will help you get a feel for what you're doing and give you a better understanding of the material.

Find a mentor: If you have someone who is experienced in the area you're trying to learn, ask them for help! This can be a great way to get insights and feedback from someone who knows what they're doing.

Take an online course: Many great online courses are out there that can help you learn new skills. Choose one that looks interesting to you and commit to actually doing the work.

Read a book: Sometimes, the best way to learn something is to read about it. Reading can assist you in gaining a deeper understanding of the material.

Observe others: Another good way to learn is by observing others. If you can't do the thing yourself, see if you can watch someone else do it. This can give you a good idea of what you need to do and how to do it.

Role playing: Another way to get experience is by role playing. This can be a great way to practice new skills and learn how to apply them in a real-world setting. If you can, find a friend or family member who will be willing to help you roleplay different scenarios. This can be a great way to learn and have some fun at the same time!

Consider different scenarios in your everyday life that might trigger you, such as dealing with a difficult customer service representative or going on a first date. Have your partner play the role of the other person in the scenario and practice using the techniques you're learning. Role playing can give you great hands-on experience without having to actually deal with the real-world consequences (just yet, anyway).

Experience By Reflecting

In addition to getting experience by doing, it's also important to reflect on your experiences. This helps you understand what you're doing and why you're doing it. It also allows you to learn from your mistakes and make adjustments as needed.

To reflect on your experiences, you can:

Keep a journal: This is a great way to document your

experiences and track your progress over time. Write down what you did, what you learned, and how you felt about it. Did it work? Do you need to make any changes?

Talk to someone: Another great way to reflect on your experiences is to talk to someone about them. This could be a friend, family member, mentor, or therapist. Talking about your experiences can help you process them and gain new insights.

Do a post-mortem: After you've completed a project or goal, take some time to reflect on what went well and what you could improve for the future. This can help you learn from your mistakes and make adjustments for next time.

Make a plan: Once you've reflected on your experiences, make a plan for how you want to proceed. What do you want to do differently? What do you want to keep doing? What do you want to stop doing? Having a plan will help you make the changes you need to make.

Making It a Habit

It's important to make reflection and experience a habit. If you only do it occasionally, you won't get the full benefits, but if you make it a regular part of your life, you'll be able to reap the rewards.

Here are a few tips for making it a habit:

Set aside time each day or week: Dedicate some time each day or week to reflection and experience. This doesn't have to be a lot of time, but it should be enough that you can really focus on what you're doing.

Make it a priority: Don't let other things impede your reflection and experience time. This is important work, so make sure you give it the attention it deserves.

Be consistent: The key to making anything a habit is consistency. So make sure you're consistently setting aside time for reflection and experience.

Be patient: Don't expect results overnight. It takes time to reflect and experience a habit. But if you stick with it, you'll eventually get there.

Reward yourself: Give yourself a pat on the back when you make progress with reflection and experience. This will help you stay motivated and keep going.

Why Is Experience Important?

Experience helps you learn and grow. It allows you to try new activities, make mistakes, and learn from them. It also allows you to develop new skills and knowledge. All of this is essential for personal and professional development.

Experience is hands-on learning. This differs from theoretical learning, which is what you do in school or from a book. Hands-on learning allows you to apply what you're learning to real-world situations, which is important because it allows you to see how the theories and concepts you're learning about actually work in practice.

As helpful as it is to read and learn, practicing an exercise in real-time can help you make the connection between the theory and real life. Experience is also important because it allows you to build confidence. The more you do something, the more confident you'll become. This is true for everything from public speaking to job interviews.

Finally, experience is important because it allows you to make connections. When you meet new people and try new things, you make connections you wouldn't have otherwise. These connections can lead to new opportunities and experiences.

Making the Most of Experience

Now that you know why experience is important, it's time to learn how to make the most of it. Here are a few tips:

Be open to new experiences: Don't be afraid to try new things. The more experiences you have, the more you'll learn and grow.

Be patient: Learning from experience takes time. Don't expect to become an expert overnight. Just be patient and keep at it.

Be persistent: If you're not having success with one experience, don't give up. Try something else or approach it from a different angle.

Be reflective: After each experience, take some time to reflect on what happened. What went well? What could have gone better? What did you learn?

Be thankful: Don't forget to be thankful for the experiences you have, even the tough ones. They're all helping you grow and learn.

Measuring Your Success

It's important to measure your success when working on personal or professional development. This will help you track your progress and see how far you've come.

To measure your success, you can start by setting goals. This could be a long-term goal, like getting a promotion, or a short-term goal, like completing a project. Another way to measure success is by looking at your accomplishments. This could be things like awards, accolades, or accomplishments at work.

Finally, you can measure success by looking at your growth. This could be things like skills you've learned, knowledge you've gained, or new experiences you've had. You can measure your growth by keeping a journal or a blog, or by tracking your progress over time.

No matter how you measure it, it's important to keep track of your progress. This will help you stay motivated and on track.

Tips for Success

To increase your chances of success with personal or professional development, here are a few tips:

Set goals: Having specific goals to work towards will help you stay on track. Make sure your goals are realistic and achievable.

Get a coach or mentor: A coach or mentor can help you learn new skills, stay motivated, and overcome challenges.

Find a role model: Find someone who has done what you want to do and learn from them.

Take action: Don't just sit around and wait for things to happen. Get out there and make things happen.

Be patient: Change takes time. Don't expect to see results overnight. Just keep at it and be patient.

Making the most of experience is important for personal and professional development. Be open to new experiences, be patient, be persistent, be reflective, and be thankful. Measure your success by setting goals, looking at your accomplishments, or tracking your growth. And finally, don't forget to take action and be patient.

By following these tips, you'll be well on your way to making the most of your experience. So get out there and start learning!

Key Takeaways

- Experience is important for personal and professional development. It helps you learn new skills, make connections, and grow as a person.

- The more hands-on you are, the more you'll learn, grow, and use what you've learned in the future.

- To make the most of your experience, be open to new things, practice being patient, persistent, reflective, and thankful.

- Set goals, review your accomplishments, or track your growth to measure your success.

- Last but not least, don't forget to take action and be patient. Change doesn't occur overnight, but if you keep putting in the effort and praise yourself for the progress you've made, you'll feel better about the process.

Chapter 11

You Are Not Alone

Our stresses, anxieties, pains and problems arise because we do not see the world, others or even ourselves as worthy of love.
—Prem Prakash

The world is an enormous place. Especially with social media right at your fingertips, you have access to connect with anyone at any time. However, it's not uncommon to feel lost, scared, and alone in this big world. It is easy to think that you are the only person feeling this way or that you are the only one struggling with your thoughts, emotions, and behaviors.

It's easy to feel like you are the only person going through a certain experience and it's hard to reach out for help, but it's important to remember that you are not alone. In this chapter, you will learn:

- The importance of socializing.

- Skills you can practice to be more social.

- How to reframe your thoughts to remember you have people by your side willing to help.

The Importance of Socializing

By nature, humans are social creatures. We are meant to interact and connect with others. In fact, just being in the presence of someone else can have a positive impact on your mood and wellbeing. When you feel alone, it's difficult to cope with your thoughts and emotions. You may start to believe that you are the only one who feels a certain way or that only you are struggling and your situation is unique to you only. This can lead to feeling isolated, which can make it even harder to cope.

You are not alone in your thoughts, emotions, or experience and other people are out there who feel the same way you do. There are other people who understand what you're going through. Many people surround you who can offer support and understanding.

If you're feeling alone, reach out to someone you're comfortable opening up to. Share your thoughts and feelings. Let them know what you're going through. Ask for their support. Just knowing that someone is there for you can make a big difference.

If you don't have anyone to talk to, many options are still available. Many helplines and online support groups are accessible to you so you can get the help you want or need.

These can be a great resource for finding understanding and support.

When you're struggling with mental health, it's easy to feel like you're an outcast. You might feel like you're the problem and have to fix yourself to be "better." However, by engaging in social interactions and practicing healthy ways of relating to others, you can feel the healing effect of the support and love around you.

CBT and Socializing

CBT can be done in a solo, partner, or family setting. It can also be done in a group setting. Group therapy can be a great way to connect with others who are going through similar experiences. It can provide support, understanding, and friendship. Working in group therapy can allow you to see other people share your experiences. You can work with others to find new ways of coping with your thoughts and emotions. You can practice with the group and receive feedback in a safe and supportive environment.

Some CBT exercises that can help are:

Identifying and challenging negative thoughts: When you're feeling alone, it's easy to spiral into negative thinking. You might start to believe that you're the only one feeling this way or that you're the only one struggling. This can lead to feeling isolated and make it even harder to cope. To overcome this, you challenge those negative thoughts and remind yourself that people are available and willing to help you. Other people are out there who share your experiences or want to help you, even if life doesn't seem that way.

Role-playing: This can be a great way to practice healthy social interactions. You can role-play with someone you trust or in a group setting. This can help you to practice new ways of interacting with others and can help to build confidence. The more confidence you have, the more you'll interact, which will help you realize you have more people in your corner than you realize.

Social skills training: You can learn and practice many social skills that will help you in your relationships, such as assertiveness, effective communication, and conflict resolution. Practicing these skills can help you socialize in a more positive and effective way.

DBT and Socializing

DBT tends to be more of a group setting. This is because the focus is on learning and practicing new skills. DBT skills groups can allow you to connect with people who are facing similar experiences. It can provide support, understanding, and friendship.

Working in a DBT skills group can allow you to see that you are not alone in your thoughts and experiences. By working with others, you can learn and practice new ways of coping through your experiences. You can practice with other people who are sharing similar struggles and receive feedback in a supportive environment.

Some DBT exercises that can help are:

Interpersonal effectiveness skills: These skills can help you interact with others in a more positive and effective way.

Mindfulness: This can help you be present in the moment and focus on your thoughts and feelings.

Distress tolerance skills: These skills can help you cope with difficult thoughts and emotions in a more effective way.

Interpersonal effectiveness skills are a critical part of DBT. This skill is broken into three parts: objective effectiveness, relationship effectiveness, and self-respect effectiveness. For each part, there is an acronym that outlines the steps to take in order to be effective.

For objective effectiveness, you can use the acronym DEAR MAN. According to Therapistaid, DEAR MAN stands for:

Describe: Describe the situation as objectively as possible.

Express: Express your feelings and needs in a clear and concise way.

Assert: Assert yourself in a way that is respectful and clear.

Reinforce: Explain how or why the outcome you want will be positive and reward the person when you receive what you want. This could be as simple as a bright smile and a cheerful "thank you!"

Mindful: Be aware of your tone and body language and try to keep them both calm.

Appear confident: Even if you don't feel confident, try to appear as such. This will help the other person to take you more seriously. Make eye contact and be firm in what you say.

Negotiate: If possible, try to come to a compromise that will benefit both parties.

For relationship effectiveness, the acronym you can use is GIVE. According to Therapistaid, GIVE stands for:

Gentle: Use a calm and kind voice when you're talking to the other person.

Interested: Be interested in what the other person has to say and show it through your body language and facial expressions.

Validate: Try to see the situation from the other person's perspective and validate their feelings. This doesn't mean that you agree with them, but it does show that you understand where they're coming from.

Easygoing: Don't be confrontational and try to be flexible in your thinking.

For self-respect effectiveness, the acronym you can use is FAST. According to Therapistaid, FAST stands for:

Fair: Be fair to yourself and to the other person. Don't try to take advantage of the situation or manipulate the other person.

Apologize: If you've done something wrong, apologize. This shows that you're willing to take responsibility for your actions.

Stick to your values: Don't compromise your values or beliefs in order to please the other person. This will only lead to you feeling resentful later on.

Truthful: Be honest with yourself and with the other person. This doesn't mean that you have to share everything, but don't hide your true feelings or intentions.

Both CBT and DBT can be beneficial for those struggling with mental health. They can both provide support, understanding, and friendship. You can learn different coping techniques to deal with your thoughts and emotions so you can feel more in control. If you are struggling with mental health, consider seeking a CBT or DBT group. There is help and support available.

Remember, the negative feelings that come with mental health are temporary, but are convincing. Those thoughts ruminating in your mind can have a hold on you, but they do not have to.

While this experience is normal, it's also unhealthy. However, CBT and DBT can help you manage those thoughts in a more effective way. The principles teach you that you are in control of your thoughts and emotions. Practice healthy coping mechanisms. Seek support. You got this. With support, understanding, and friendship, you can overcome anything.

Key Takeaways

- Humans are social creatures by nature. You need connection and support from others, especially when you're going through tough times.

- Mental health can be a difficult thing to manage, but you are not alone. Remember, your thoughts might tell you that you have no one, but that's not true.

- CBT and DBT can help you manage your thoughts and emotions in a more effective way. They both focus on teaching new skills and providing support.

- CBT and DBT can both provide support, understanding, new skills, and enhanced friendship.

- Those techniques can also help you practice unique methods to cope with your thoughts and emotions.

CHAPTER 12

Breath in Peace, Exhale and Let Go

Your mind will answer most questions if you learn to relax and wait for the answer.
—William S. Burroughs

Being aware of your emotions, thoughts, and feelings, and how they affect you is the first step to regulating your emotions. This awareness can be a good and bad thing. It can be good because you are more in tune with how you are feeling and can catch yourself before your emotions get the best of you. However, it can be bad because you may dwell on negative emotions and thoughts, but because you'll do anything to fix it, you may wind up feeling overwhelmed or stressed. This is why the next step is learning how to control and manage these emotions so they don't take over your life.

When it feels like the weight of the world is on your shoulders and you're about to snap, it's important to have some go-to techniques to help you relax and de-stress. One way to do this is through mindfulness practices that can help regulate day-to-day outburst of emotions or emotional numbness.

The goal of this chapter is to provide you with some mindfulness-based techniques that can help you cope with your emotions in a more constructive way. In this chapter, you will learn about:

- What mindfulness is.

- The benefits of mindfulness.

- How to practice mindfulness.

- Mindful-based techniques for managing emotions.

What Is Mindfulness?

Mindfulness is defined as the quality or state of being aware of something (Merriam-Webster, 2010). In other words, mindfulness is about being aware of what is happening in the present moment, without judging it as good or bad. When you are mindful, you observe your thoughts and emotions, but you don't allow them to consume you.

This can be a hard task because our natural tendency is to judge our experiences as good or bad. For example, if you are feeling sad, you may judge yourself for being sad and try to push the feeling away. Mindfulness allows you to be with your emotions, without judging them.

Additionally, mindfulness can be difficult because your brain goes into auto pilot often. This means that you are not really aware of what you are thinking and feeling because your brain literally has a mind of its own. To be mindful, you need to be aware of your thoughts and feelings as they are happening, which means you have to redirect your attention on purpose.

This can be a challenge, especially because redirecting your attention takes effort and needs to be done constantly. Every time your mind wanders, you would need to redirect your attention to the present. It gets easier with practice, but you may not always realize when your brain goes into autopilot mode, especially when you're a beginner, which can make the benefits difficult to obtain initially.

Mindfulness has many benefits, both for your mental and physical health. Some of the benefits include

- Reduced stress
- Anxiety relief
- Depression relief
- Improved sleep quality
- Better focus and concentration
- Increased self-awareness

- Enhanced well-being

How to Practice Mindfulness

You can practice being mindful in many ways, but the basic principle is always the same: focus your attention on what's occurring in the present moment and notice your thoughts and feelings without judging them as good or bad. Many activities can help you practice mindfulness, but some of the most common ways include:

Meditation: Meditation is a practice that allows you to focus your attention on the present moment. There are many different types of meditation, but the goal is always the same: to focus your attention on your breathing and its sensations. To observe your thoughts and feelings without judging or reacting to them. For meditation practices, you can try:

Breathing meditation: Sit in a comfortable position with your eyes closed. Focus your attention on your breath and its sensations. Notice when your mind wanders and redirect your attention back to your breath.

Body scan: Get into a comfortable position and focus your attention on different parts of your body, notice any sensations you feel.

Walking meditation: Walk at a slow pace and focus your

attention on your breath and the sensation of your feet hitting the ground.

Mindful eating: Another way to practice mindfulness is to focus your attention on your food and the act of eating. Pay attention to the taste, texture, and smell of your food. Be aware of when your mind wanders so you can redirect your attention back to your food.

Yoga: Yoga is a physical practice that involves moving your body, focusing your attention on your breath, and being present in the moment.

Focusing on your senses: Pay attention to the sights, sounds, smells, tastes, and sensations you experience.

Progressive muscle relaxation: Tense and relax different muscle groups in your body when you're in a comfortable position.

Labeling your thoughts: As you notice your thoughts, label them as "thinking" without judging them as good or bad.

When you first start practicing mindfulness, it may be difficult to focus your attention on the present moment. Your mind may wander often, and you may find it hard to concentrate. This is normal, but with practice, it will get easier. Eventually, you will be more mindful of your everyday life and experience the benefits of mindfulness.

Below is a progressive muscle relaxation exercise for you to put your mindful skills to the test.

Progressive Muscle Relaxation Exercise

Follow the directions and answer the reflection questions after you've completed the exercise. Progressive muscle relaxation is a stress-reduction technique that involves tensing and relaxing different muscle groups in the body. The goal is to achieve a state of deep relaxation.

1. Start by sitting or lying down in a comfortable position. Close your eyes and take a few deep breaths to relax your body.

2. Begin with your feet and slowly tense and then relax each muscle group. Work your way up to your calves, thighs, hips, abdomen, chest, arms, hands, neck, jaw, and face.

3. Tense each muscle group for 5-10 seconds and then relax for 30 seconds.

4. Visualize each muscle group relaxing as you go.

5. Once you've gone through all the muscle groups, take a few deep breaths and notice how your body feels.

Reflection Questions

- How did you feel during the exercise?
- What thoughts went through your mind while you were

doing the exercise?

- Did you notice any changes in your body after the exercise?

- How do you think this exercise can help you in the future?

Mindfulness-Based Techniques for Managing Emotions

Once you have learned how to be mindful of your thoughts and feelings, you can use mindfulness to manage your emotions. Mindfulness-based techniques can help you to:

Accept your emotions without judgment: When you're experiencing negative emotions, it can be tempting to judge yourself for feeling that way. Mindfulness can help you accept your emotions without judgment and allow them to pass.

Observe your emotions without reacting to them: It's natural to want to react to your emotions, but mindfulness can help you observe them without reacting. If you can prolong your reaction, you can avoid making the situation worse.

Manage your emotions healthily: Mindfulness can help you manage your emotions healthily by teaching you how to deal with them in the moment.

A good deal of different mindful-based techniques can help you manage your emotions. Some of the most common techniques include:

Breathing: Taking slow, deep breaths can help you calm down and focus on the present moment.

Visualization: Visualizing a calm place or situation can help you relax and feel more in control.

Journaling: You can understand your thoughts and emotions by journalism, which can help you manage them healthily. If you're struggling to write directly from or about your experiences, you can opt to use a guided journal instead. Guided journals provide prompts, information, or relatable stories to help you get started and reflect upon.

Mindfulness meditation: As you learned earlier, mindfulness meditation can help you concentrate on the present moment and acknowledge your thoughts and feelings.

Guided relaxation: Listening to a guided relaxation can help you relax your body and mind.

Exercise: Exercise can be a great mindful practice and you reap the benefits of keeping your body in shape. Exercising requires a mind-muscle connection (especially when lifting weights) and one of the best ways to accomplish that is by focusing on your breath and the sensation of your muscles working.

Spending time in nature: Research has shown that spending time in nature can help to reduce stress and anxiety. Even if it's a short walk outside, or eating lunch under a tree, being in nature can help you feel more relaxed and connected to the world around you. Focus on the scenery in front of you and the surrounding sounds.

Art: Mindfully completing a task such as art can help you focus on the present moment and express your emotions creatively. You can paint, draw, color, pottery, or do any other type of art that you enjoy. Art will help you focus on the present, which will distract you from the turmoil within, and is a productive way to be creative.

Dancing: Dancing is a great way to let loose, have fun, and get some exercise. When you dance, focus on the music and the movement of your body. Let go of your inhibitions and allow yourself to enjoy the moment.

Cognitive restructuring: This technique involves challenging and changing the negative thoughts that contribute to your stress and anxiety.

CBT and Mindfulness

CBT techniques can be used with mindfulness practices to help you regulate your emotions and stay in the present moment. One CBT technique that can regulate emotions is deep breathing. Deep breathing helps to calm the body and mind and can be used in any situation where you are feeling overwhelmed or tense. To do deep breathing, simply inhale deeply through your nose, filling your lungs with air.

Then exhale slowly through your mouth, letting all the air out. Repeat this for several minutes until you feel more relaxed. Another CBT technique that can manage emotions is cognitive restructuring, where you challenge and change the negative beliefs that add to your stress and anxiety. For example, if you are anxious about an upcoming event, you may think thoughts such as, *I'm going to fail*, or *I'm not good enough*. These thoughts can contribute to your anxiety and make the situation seem more daunting than it actually is.

To challenge these thoughts, you can ask yourself questions such as, *What evidence do I have that I will fail? Or what are some other probable outcomes?* This will help you see the situation in a more realistic and positive light, which can reduce your anxiety. You can also use mindfulness practices such as meditation and relaxation to help you stay in the present moment and focus on your breath. This will assist you in recognizing your thoughts and emotions, which will allow you to let go of the thought processes that contribute to your anxiety.

Key Takeaways

- To regulate your emotions and practice staying in the present moment, you can use CBT and mindfulness skills together.

- Deep breathing and cognitive restructuring are two CBT techniques that can manage emotions.

- Mindfulness practices such as meditation or yoga can help you turn your attention to the present moment and focus on your breath.

- Mindfulness helps you focus on your thoughts and emotions, so you can let the negative thoughts that contribute to your angst dissipate.

- If you are feeling overwhelmed by emotions, try using some of these techniques to help you stay in the here and now so you can manage your stress and anxiety.

Conclusion

In the end, just three things matter: How well we have lived. How well we have loved. How well we have learned to let go.
—Jack Kornfield

Congratulations! You have completed *CBT and DBT for Anxiety and Pani*c. How do you feel? Have you used any skills outlined in the workbook in your daily life? If so, how did it go? If not, why not? What are your thoughts on CBT? Do you think it can help you in your day-to-day life? What are your thoughts on DBT? Do you think you can use DBT principles in your day-to-day life? DBT and CBT are great tools to have in your arsenal for managing your emotions. You can use these tools together to create a well-rounded therapeutic practice that helps you regulate your emotions and live a more balanced life.

It took some time, but when I started implementing these skills in my daily life, I really saw a difference. Not only did my relationships improve, but I found I could cope with stress and adversity in a more healthy way. I'm much older now, with more knowledge and more experience to learn from, but I still have bad days. However, these skills have helped me to manage my emotions in a more positive way. It also allowed me to realize when others were suffering like I did. This was the case with my fourteen-year-old daughter, who was recently diagnosed with anxiety and depression.

Upon entering high school, I saw a dramatic change in my once vivacious daughter. Much like me at her age, she became withdrawn, didn't want to go to school, and would often cry for no apparent reason. My wife was distraught and worried. With suicide becoming more and more popular, the thought of losing our daughter in that way was unbearable. However, I had a toolkit full of skills that I could use to help her. Between her personal therapist and nightly sessions with me, she was soon on the road to recovery, and much more quickly than I was at her age. CBT and DBT have saved my life and my daughter's life. I am eternally grateful.

DBT and CBT are lifelong skills you can use to manage your emotions. It takes time and practice to master them, but it is worthwhile. These skills have helped me to live a more balanced life and I hope they can do the same for you. Below is a quick review of the skills you have learned in this workbook.

DBT is a set of skills that you can use to manage your emotions. The four modules in DBT are mindfulness, distress tolerance, interpersonal effectiveness, and emotion regulation. The first step is to realize your emotions. You can do this by noticing how your body feels when you experience an emotion. The second step is to label your emotions. This helps you to understand what you are feeling.

The third step is to accept your emotions. This means that you acknowledge your emotions without judgment. The fourth step is to regulate your emotions. This means that you manage your emotions in a healthy and productive way. Distress tolerance and interpersonal effectiveness skills are used in order to manage your emotions and develop more positive relationships.

CBT is a set of skills that you can use to manage your thoughts. The modules for this skill include identifying and challenging negative thoughts, changing negative thinking patterns, and developing positive thinking skills. The first step to managing your thoughts is to identify the negative thoughts that are causing you distress. Challenging these thoughts is the second step. This means that you examine the evidence for and against your thoughts.

The third step is to change your thinking patterns. This means that you find more positive and productive ways of thinking. The fourth step is to develop positive thinking skills, so you learn how to reframe your thoughts to be more positive.

One therapy technique is about identifying and challenging your emotions, while the other focuses on your thoughts. However, it's been proven that the two are interconnected. What you think affects how you feel and vice versa. That's why it's important to learn both CBT and DBT skills. Both CBT and DBT are skills you can use to manage your emotions, but in different ways. By using these techniques together, you can create a well-rounded therapeutic practice that assists you with regulating your emotions so you can be more balanced in life.

Although they focus on different areas, you can use each technique to complement each other and create a more comprehensive approach to emotional regulation. For instance, you can use the CBT module on challenging and reframing your thoughts to help you with the DBT skill of labeling your emotions. Or, you can use the DBT skill of mindfulness to help you with the CBT skill of challenging your thoughts.

CBT and DBT are two of the most popular and effective methods for emotional regulation. If you are struggling to manage your emotions, I encourage you to seek a therapist who specializes in these techniques. With the help of a professional, you can learn how to use these skills to live a more balanced life. Although these techniques are geared to help those suffering from mental health, you don't have to suffer from emotional difficulties to benefit from these skills. Anyone can use these skills to improve their emotional well-being, live in the moment, and enhance their relationships.

Learning two different techniques may seem daunting, but it's worth it to invest in your emotional health. These skills will help you regulate your emotions, cope with difficult situations, and live a more balanced life. Here are a few tips to keep in mind as you start learning these skills:

1. Start with one skill at a time. Don't try to learn both CBT and DBT at the same time. Start with one skill and build

from there.

2. Find a therapist who specializes in these techniques. A therapist can help you learn and practice these skills in a safe and supportive environment.

3. Join a support group. Many CBT and DBT groups exist for you to join so you can get support and practice these skills with others.

4. Practice, practice, practice. The more you practice these skills, the better you will become at using them. Also, the more you practice, the more these techniques become natural and effortless.

5. Be patient with yourself. Learning new skills takes time and effort. Don't get discouraged if you don't see results immediately. With time and practice, you will see the benefits of these skills in your life.

Keep in mind, change is possible, but it's all about progress, not perfection. You are human and it's likely that you will make mistakes. Maybe not today or tomorrow, but practicing internal forgiveness and acceptance will make it easier for you to get back on track when you make a mistake. So, take it one day at a time and be gentle with yourself as you learn these new skills.

This book has everything you need to know. From the easy-to-read CBT and DBT techniques to worksheets, activities and exercises, this book will help you on your journey to emotional wellness! Don't wait any longer. Start your journey today!

Thank You

Before you leave, I'd just like to say, thank you so much for purchasing my book.

I spent many days and nights working on this book so I could finally put this in your hands.

So, before you leave, I'd like to ask you a small favor.

Would you please consider posting a review on the platform? Your reviews are one of the best ways to support indie authors like me, and every review counts.

Your feedback will allow me to continue writing books just like this one, so let me know if you enjoyed it and why. I read every review and I would love to hear from you.

The Ultimate Guide to Cognitive Behavioral Therapy

Website Link:
LindaHillBooks.com/cbtcourse

Scan this QR code to visit the link

Disclaimer: The CBT course serves as an educational resource and tool to enhance personal understanding and coping skills. It is crucial to consult with a qualified mental health professional before engaging in any therapeutic program, including this course. Only a trained professional can accurately diagnose and provide appropriate treatment for specific mental health conditions.

While CBT can be beneficial as a complementary approach, it should be utilized in conjunction with other forms of therapy, as determined by a licensed mental health provider. The course's material and techniques should not replace or supersede personalized treatment plans, medication, or other evidence-based interventions recommended by a mental health professional.

References

American Psychological Association. (2017). What Is Cognitive Behavioral Therapy?

American Psychological Association. https://www.apa.org/ptsd-guideline/patients-and-families/cognitive-behavioral

Carmody, J. (2020, January 10). *Why we are hard-wired to worry, and what we can do to calm down*. The Conversation. https://theconversation.com/why-we-are-hard-wired-to-worry-and-what-we-can-do-to-calm-down-127674

Center, M. R. (2020, October 28). *How to Use Both CBT and DBT for Recovery*. Midwest Recovery Center. https://www.midwestrecoverycenter.com/rehab-blog/how-to-use-both-cbt-and-dbt-for-recovery/

DBT Distress Tolerance Skills (Worksheet). (n.d.). Therapist Aid.

https://www.therapistaid.com/therapy-worksheet/dbt-distress-tolerance-skills/dbt/none

DBT Emotion Regulation Skills (Worksheet). (n.d.). Therapist Aid.

https://www.therapistaid.com/therapy-worksheet/dbt-emotion-regulation-skills/dbt/none

DBT Interpersonal Effectiveness Skills (Worksheet). (n.d.). Therapist Aid.

References

https://www.therapistaid.com/therapy-worksheet/dbt-interpersonal-effectiveness-skills

DBT Skill: ACCEPTS (Worksheet). (n.d.). Therapist Aid.

https://www.therapistaid.com/therapy-worksheet/dbt-accepts/dbt/none

DBT Skill: DEAR MAN (Worksheet). (n.d.). Therapist Aid.

https://www.therapistaid.com/therapy-worksheet/dbt-dear-man/dbt/none

Definition of MINDFULNESS. (2019). Merriam-Webster.com. https://www.merriam-webster.com/dictionary/mindfulness

Dialectical Behavior Therapy (DBT). (n.d.). Cleveland Clinic.

https://my.clevelandclinic.org/health/treatments/22838-dialectical-behavior-therapy-dbt

Dialectical Behavior Therapy: Shame, Guilt and Emotional Distress. (2015, January 4).

E D I. https://edinstitute.org/blog/2015/1/4/dialectical-behavior-therapy-shame-guilt-and-emotional-distress

Dialectical Behavioral Therapy versus Cognitive Behavioral Therapy: What's Best for Me? (2020, June 25). Suzanne Wallach. https://suzannewallach.com/blog/dbt-v-cbt/

Distress Tolerance Skills. (n.d.). Retrieved August 11, 2022, from

https://www.therapistaid.com/worksheets/dbt-distress-tolerance-skills

8 Tips to Get to the Root of Your Anxiety and Why It Matters. (2021, September 14).

Psych Central. https://psychcentral.com/anxiety/getting-to-the-root-of-your-anxiety#how-to-explore-the-causes

Family Doctor Editorial Staff. (2017, July 27). *Mental Health: Keeping Your Emotional*

Health. Familydoctor.org. https://familydoctor.org/mental-health-keeping-your-emotional-health/

Felman, A. (2021, March 23). *What causes anxiety?* Www.medicalnewstoday.com.

https://www.medicalnewstoday.com/articles/323456#summary

4 Differences Between CBT and DBT and How to Tell Which is Right for You | Skyland

Trail. (2017, August 27). Skyland Trail. https://www.skylandtrail.org/4-differences-between-cbt-and-dbt-and-how-to-tell-which-is-right-for-you/

Gotter, A. (2017, May 23). *Understanding Emotional Numbness*. Healthline; Healthline

Media. https://www.healthline.com/health/feeling-numb

How Can You Get Out Of The Depression Danger Zone? - Beachside Teen Treatment

Center. (2020, May 12). Beachside Teen Treatment Center. https://beachsideteen.com/how-can-you-get-out-of-the-depression-danger-zone/

Interpersonal Effectiveness Skills. (n.d.). Retrieved August 11, 2022, from

https://www.therapistaid.com/worksheets/dbt-interpersonal-effectiveness-skills

Lindberg, S. (2007, December 11). *What Is Emotional Numbness?* Verywell Mind;

Verywell Mind. https://www.verywellmind.com/emotional-numbing-symptoms-2797372

Linehan, M. (n.d.-a). *ABC Please Skill*. Dialectical Behavior Therapy (DBT) Tools.

https://dbt.tools/emotional_regulation/abc-please.php

Linehan, M. (n.d.-b). *STOP Skill*. Dialectical Behavior Therapy (DBT) Tools.

https://dbt.tools/emotional_regulation/stop.php

References

Mayo Clinic. (2019). *Cognitive Behavioral Therapy*. Mayoclinic.org. https://www.mayoclinic.org/tests-procedures/cognitive-behavioral-therapy/about/pac-20384610

Meissner, B. (2015, January 12). *Warning Signs and Risk Factors*. Www.samhsa.gov. https://www.samhsa.gov/find-help/disaster-distress-helpline/warning-signs-risk-factors

Nunez, K. (2020, August 10). *Progressive Muscle Relaxation: Benefits, How-To, Technique*. Healthline. https://www.healthline.com/health/progressive-muscle-relaxation#how-to-do-it

Parade. (2020, February 1). *101 Anxiety Quotes to Help You Get Through and Lift Your Spirits*. Parade: Entertainment, Recipes, Health, Life, Holidays. https://parade.com/951718/parade/anxiety-quotes/

Psychology Today. (2014). *Dialectical Behavior Therapy | Psychology Today*. https://www.psychologytoday.com/us/therapy-types/dialectical-behavior-therapy

Watson, E. (2020, August 31). *DBT vs. CBT: Understanding the Differences*. Choosing Therapy. https://www.choosingtherapy.com/dbt-vs-cbt/

What Could Happen vs. What Will Happen. (n.d.). Retrieved August 11, 2022, from

https://www.therapistaid.com/worksheets/worry-exploration-questions

Printed in Great Britain
by Amazon